# Walking the Kurrum Yallock (Plenty River)

## History, Heritage and Environment

Section 1:
Birrarung (Yarra River) to Martins Lane

---

Section 2:
Martins Lane to Yallambie

### Anne Paul

**Greensborough Historical Society**

First published by Busybird Publishing 2023

Copyright © 2023 Anne Paul and Greensborough Historical Society Inc.

**ISBN:** 978-1-922954-41-1

This work is copyright. Apart from any use permitted under the *Copyright Act 1968*, no part of this publication may be reproduced, stored in a retrieval system or transmitted in any form or by any means, electronic, mechanical, photocopying, recording or otherwise, without the prior written permission of Anne Paul and Greensborough Historical Society Inc.

The information in this book is based on the author's experiences and opinions. The author and publisher disclaim responsibility for any adverse consequences, which may result from use of the information contained herein. Permission to use any external content has been sought by the author. Any breaches will be rectified in further editions of the book.

**Front cover photo:** Plenty River near confluence with Birrarung - Photo by Anne Paul

**Back cover photo:** Plenty River Waterwatch near Old Plenty Rd Bridge, during the Millennium Drought

**Cover design:** Busybird Publishing

**Layout and typesetting:** Busybird Publishing

Busybird Publishing
2/118 Para Road
Montmorency, Victoria
Australia 3094
www.busybird.com.au

**NOTE: While most of the walk is on paved trails or footpaths, sections are on gravel or dirt tracks. Some sections are also steep.**

# Contents

About the Author     1

**Walking the Kurrum Yallock (Plenty River) History, Heritage and Environment**

*Section 1: Birrarung (Yarra River) to Martins Lane*     *3*

The Walk and Heritage Sites     10

References     30

Footprints on the Landscape     32

*Section 2: Martins Lane to Yallambie*     *39*

The Walk and Heritage Sites     44

References     65

Images of Plenty Bridge (Golf Club) Hotel     66

# About the Author

Anne Paul has been leading walks along the Yallambie – Lower Plenty section of the Kurrum Yallock for many years. Informal at first, with a few notes on key sites, ongoing research and collaboration has resulted in a comprehensive knowledge of the lower section of the River.

As a founding member of Greensborough Historical Society, Anne has brought this knowledge to the community through a series of presentations and articles about the River's heritage.

Anne has also been an active volunteer with the Friends of the Plenty River for over 20 years. The Friends have carried out indigenous revegetation and weed control, in conjunction with Banyule City Council and Melbourne Water. Through this work she has acquired a hands-on knowledge of some special places along the River and has interwoven this with the heritage narrative.

# Acknowledgements

Thanks to the following people for their assistance with the research and preparation of these notes.

- Russell Yeoman and Jim Connor – Eltham District Historical Society
- Andrew Lucas – Friends of Yarra Valley Parks
- Sue Ballantyne, Noel Withers and John Gibson – Greensborough Historical Society
- Ian Bryant – research on Robert Hoddle's Field Survey notes and producing the heritage walk maps
- Ian McLachlan – site information and photos

Greensborough Historical Society acknowledges the Wurundjeri Woi-wurrung people as traditional custodians of the land and we pay respect to all Elders, past, present and emerging, who have resided in the area and been an integral part of the region's history.

# Walking the Kurrum Yallock (Plenty River)

### History, Heritage and Environment

# Section 1:
# Birrarung (Yarra River) to Martins Lane

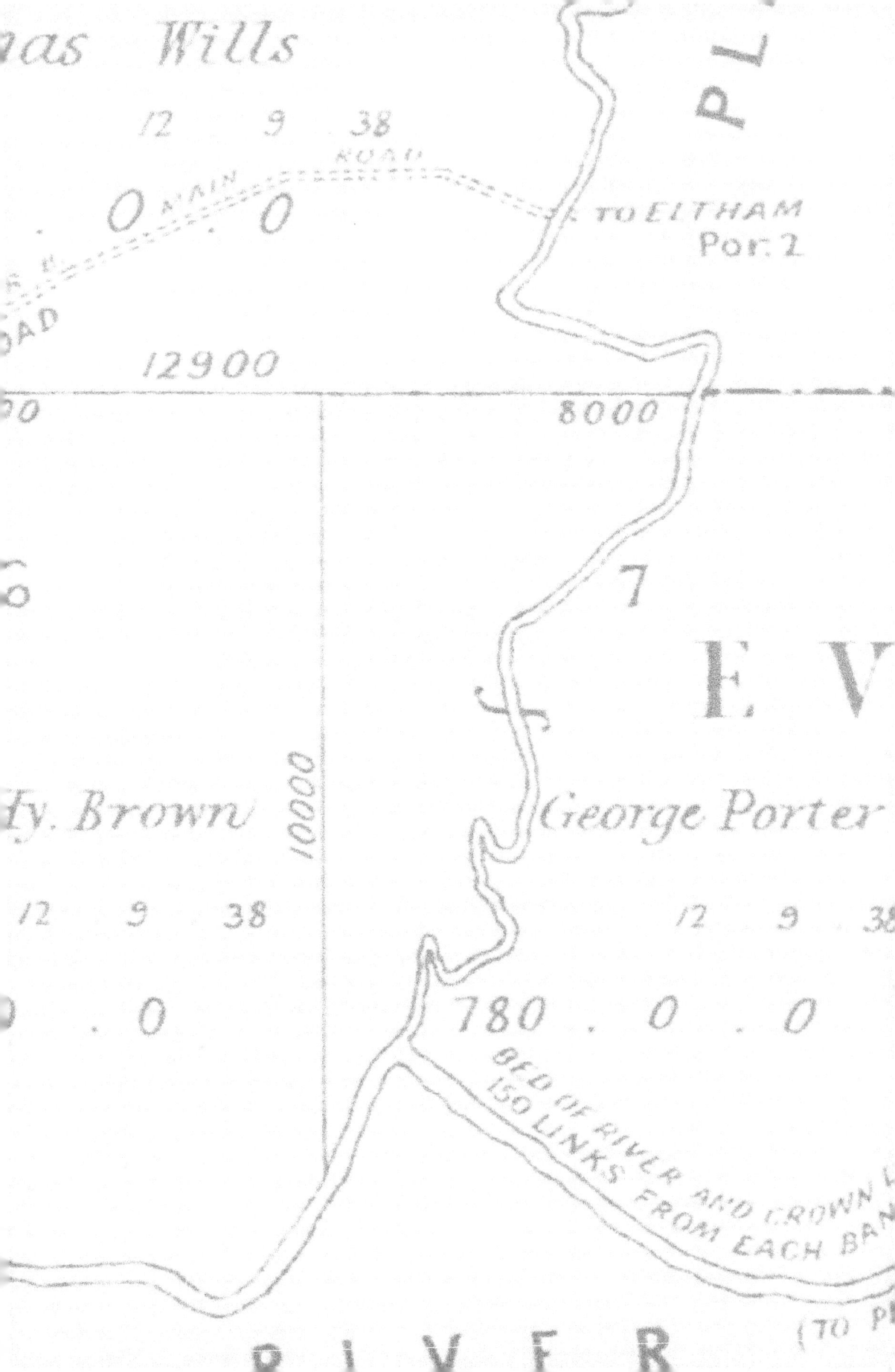

# Birrarung (Yarra River) to Martins Lane

Kurrum Yallock, the Plenty River has its source in the foothills of the Great Dividing Range near Mt Disappointment. It flows through the township of Whittlesea and the outer suburbs of Mernda, Doreen and South Morang, then on to suburban Greensborough, Yallambie, Viewbank and Lower Plenty before joining Birrarung, the Yarra River.

The Plenty River and Valley is contained within a continuous corridor of public land, managed by either Parks Victoria or Local Government Councils from Bridge Inn Rd, Mernda. The final section flows through the privately owned Rosanna Golf Course, then public land for the last few metres.

The confluence is accessible via the Main Yarra Trail, from either Bonds Road or Somerset Avenue.

**Plenty River Trail**

The Plenty River Trail starts in Viewbank, as a branch off the Main Yarra Trail, near Banyule Flats Reserve. The Trail deviates away from the Plenty River in this lower section and passes through Parks Victoria land on the west of the River to Martins Lane.

The Trail then travels north along the Plenty Valley to Greensborough and terminates just north of the Maroondah Aqueduct Pipe Bridge. The Trail is to connect to the Plenty Gorge Parklands Trail, via the Pipe Bridge creating a continuous trail from the Yarra River to Bridge Inn Rd, Mernda.

**The Plenty River**

The Plenty River was given its name by Joseph Tice Gellibrand, of the Port Phillip Association in February 1836, in view of its high flow of water. It is Melbourne's third river, after the Yarra and Maribyrnong. In his 1837 field survey notes, Robert Hoddle referred to the Plenty River by the names Willis's Creek, Yarra Yarra Rivulet and $3^{rd'}$, meaning the third waterway surveyed.

Jim Poulter, who has analysed Wurundjeri Elder William Barak's 1888 Coranderrk Narrative, confirms the Indigenous name of the Plenty River is Kurrum Yallock, meaning muddy creek.

> "Barak's third named location, Muddy Creek, is more obscure unless you are aware that the Woiwurung word for 'muddy' is 'Kurrum'. Also the word for creek is 'Yallock'. 'Kurrum Yallock' …. is the original name of the Plenty River."

(Poulter, J. 2020)

Yan-yan (child or young man) is the Indigenous name for the confluence of the Plenty with the Yarra.

**First Nations Heritage**

The Plenty River and Valley are part of the territory of the Wurundjeri-willam, a clan of the Kulin Nation. Their territory extends across the Birrarung Valley and tributaries. Wurundjeri people take their name from the word *wurun* meaning Manna Gum which is common along Birrarung and *djeri*, a grub found in the trees. (Wurundjeri Cultural Heritage website, 2021)

The confluence of the Yarra and Plenty has likely significant First Nations heritage, with stone artefacts found nearby in 1970s and oral history indicating ceremonies were performed there.

They used the Yarra and Plenty Rivers for fishing and hunting, the trees for bark and the grounds for camping and ceremony. Their traditional life changed forever with the arrival of the Europeans.

The Assistant Protector of Aborigines, William Thomas, reported to the Select Committee of the Legislative Council on the Aborigines 1858-1859 that an area near the junction of the Plenty and Yarra Rivers was the site of corroborees commemorating religious or traditional events which lasted for 10 nights and involved strange bark figures.

> "Near the junction of the River Plenty with the Yarra, were for ten nights continued corroberries (sic), all commemorating religious or traditionary events, when huge and strange figures … painted on large sheets of bark … were placed and borne in the corroberries (sic). I have seen many since then, but have not the materials, I was anxious to preserve those of the Plenty, but while in Melbourne, one day, parties came with two drays and took the huge sheets of bark away for roofing purposes."

(LC Report s.51, p.62)

Archaeologist Fiona Weaver in her 1991 survey along the Lower Plenty River notes:

> "European settlement had a significant impact on the indigenous archaeological landscape. Many settlers collected artefacts from their land and either kept them or gave them away..."

and to her knowledge

> "there are virtually no public collections from this area."

She identified scar trees near Seymour Road and on Rosanna Golf Course, along with several artefact scatters. (Weaver, F. 1991)

The majority of vegetation in the Plenty River Valley was cleared for agriculture by Europeans, leaving only a narrow riparian strip along the river bank and some shade trees.

There are few known references to First Nations people in the Lower Plenty area, in the records of the early Europeans. In his 1837 diary, Lower Plenty squatter James Willis makes one reference to scarcity of game, due to their hunting. (Willis, J. 1837)

### Early European Squatters

The Lower Plenty area was first explored and occupied by squatters and their shepherds - John Nicholas Wood on the west side in 1836 and Edward and James Willis on the east in April 1837.

### Crown Land Survey and Sales

The area was surveyed and subdivided into Crown Land Portions 6 and 7, Parish of Keelbundora, County of Bourke, by Robert Hoddle and William Wedge Darke and their survey team in July - August 1837. The land was sold at auction to Richard H. Browne and George Porter as part of the first land sales in Port Phillip District on 12 September 1838.

# The Walk and Heritage Sites

The walk starts on the Main Yarra Trail, at either the Somerset Drive or Bonds Road car park. It follows a circuit around the lower part of the Plenty River and along the Main Yarra Trail, crossing the confluence of the Plenty with the Yarra River.

These notes are clockwise from the Somerset Drive car park but can be followed in reverse from Bonds Road. The walk takes approximately 3 – 4 hours.

The walk travels up the Plenty River Trail to Martins Lane. It then turns down Seymour Road and crosses the Plenty River on the Henty Road Bridge, onto Cleveland Avenue then Stawell Road. The final part of the walk travels down Bonds Road, linking back onto the Main Yarra Trail.

As much of this part of the Plenty River is located within the privately owned Rosanna Golf Club, the majority of the walk is on Parks Victoria shared trails or public roadways.

**West Side of the Plenty River**

*Walk east from Somerset Drive car park, along the Main Yarra Trail*

*Turn left onto the Plenty River Trail and walk up Viewbank Hill*

There are good views of the Yarra River and Banyule Billabong. At the top of Viewbank Hill look west to the Assisi Aged Care Centre in Rosanna Road, formerly the 1920s Sisters of Mercy Novitiate Convent, then further south to Banyule House in Buckingham Drive.

**Site 1: Early European Squatter John Nicholas Wood's Sheep Run 1836-37**

John Nicholas Wood was the son of Captain William Wood of Van Diemen's Land. He came to Port Phillip with his sheep and after initially going to Werribee, established his sheep run on the west side of the Plenty River in late 1836. He had a hut near present day Banyule Tennis Courts, as noted in Hoddle's survey notes 24 and 26 July 1837, as *'Mr Wood's House.'*

## Crown Land Sales – Portion 6

Portion 6 extended north from the Yarra River to Martins Lane. It was auctioned on 12 September 1838 and purchased by Richard H. Browne for £1,334. Browne called his estate Heidelberg. Like most owners of these estates, Browne had other pastoral interests around Port Phillip District. He was characterised as a *'dandy gent cashing in on the land boom.'* He did not stay long at Heidelberg, subdividing Portion 6 in 1839, which returned him a handsome profit. (Bolderwood, R. 1896)

## Banyule Estate

Joseph Hawdon purchased 750 acres of Portion 6 and established Banyule Estate. He had moved cattle overland from Sydney in 1836 and was a successful breeder and trader. Banyule Estate gained fame for its gothic style mansion 'Banyule House', which was constructed by Hawdon in 1846. The House is heritage listed as one of the oldest surviving houses in Victoria. It is located in Buckingham Drive, Heidelberg, overlooking the Banyule Flats and Swamp.

In 1942 Banyule Estate operated as a dairy and stud farm before being sold to property developer Stanley Korman in 1958, with much of the Estate then developed for housing.

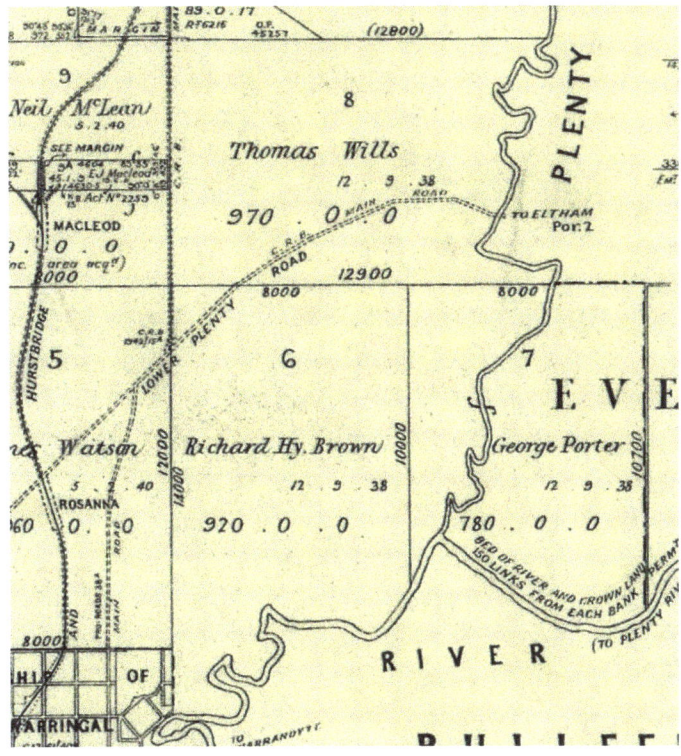

Map of Portions 6 and 7 - Parish of Keelbundora 1837. Source: State Library Victoria

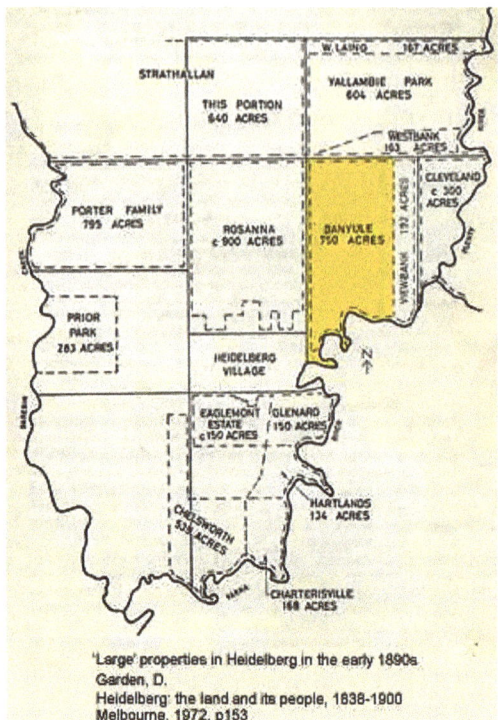

**Banyule and Viewbank subdivisions of Portion 6**
From – Garden, D. Heidelberg the Land and its People, 1972, p155

In the 1970s Banyule House was renovated to provide a Gallery for the National Gallery of Victoria's Heidelberg School Collection. In 1995, the property was sold and returned to private ownership. It was sold for $5.2M in 2015 then again in 2019, for an undisclosed amount following an unsuccessful attempt to commercialise the site.

**Banyule House 2015**

Heidelberg School artist Walter Withers painted *Tranquil Winter* in 1895 from a viewpoint near the old farmhouse he lived in on Banyule Estate, now in Walker Court, as well as other local scenes.

Tranquil Winter by Walter Withers 1895 Source: National Gallery Victoria

### Viewbank and Viewbank Homestead

Pastoralist James Williamson purchased the adjoining 192 acres of Portion 6 in 1839, naming it Viewbank, after a property in Scotland. In 1841 Williamson was deeply in debt and sold Viewbank to wealthy squatter and Port Phillip Society member Dr Robert Martin in 1842. (Peters, S. 1996)

Viewbank is significant as one of the earliest pastoral settlements on the Yarra that remained a farming property until the 1990s. It is now part of the Banyule Flats Reserve, managed by Parks Victoria and contains several significant heritage sites.

*Continue walking along the Trail to the area with trees and signage*

### Site 2: Site of Viewbank Homestead

The site comprises the remains of Viewbank Homestead - a house constructed c.1839 and extended in 1850, with remnant plantings and remains of outbuildings, gateposts and archaeological deposits.

Viewbank Homestead was one of the first grand homesteads built on the outskirts of Melbourne.

Built by James Williamson, it was originally a four room house. The 1841 census recorded *"a genteel weather board residence, detached stables, coach house and gardens."* It was renovated by Dr Martin into a large single-storey homestead in the 1850s which he called 'Heidelberg House'. The farm was fenced and used for grazing dairy cattle.

The Martin family moved to Viewbank in 1843 and spent many years there. They were described as *"typical of the early, middle-class immigrants who brought their gentility and privilege with them to the colony."* Dr Martin died in 1874 and with other family tragedy the family drifts away from Viewbank. The house and the land was leased for farming, including to Joseph Bond in 1877 and dairy farmer Thomas Robinson from 1911 – 1920. (Hayes, S. 2014; Peters, S. 1996)

Viewbank Homestead was demolished in the early 1920s. The House had fallen into disrepair and was unoccupied apart from a caretaker. Locals believed it was haunted with the orange grove and garden in ruin and paddocks covered in briars.

Between 1996 and 1999, Heritage Victoria conducted three excavations at the site with archaeologists from Melbourne, La Trobe and Flinders Universities, students and community volunteers. They uncovered the stone foundations of the house, remnants of hand-made brick walls and fireplaces. Artefacts found included children's toys, coins, gaming tokens, thimbles and pins, servant's bells, fragments of marble fireplaces and pieces of decorated plaster cornices.

Sarah Hayes in her report *Good Taste, Fashion, Luxury: A Genteel Melbourne Family and their Rubbish* provides a detailed interpretation of the site. She also refers to a *"large Wurundjeri settlement being located at the junction of the Plenty and Yarra Rivers,"* citing a 1981 report on a tip trench excavation for the Archaeological and Anthropological Society of Victoria, in 1980.

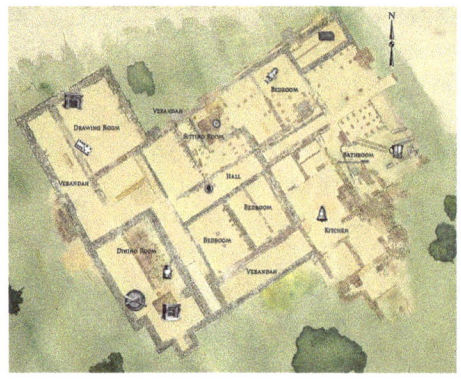

**Floor plan Viewbank Homestead**     **1990s Archaeological Dig**

## Site 3: Bartram Dairy Farm and Silos

Viewbank was owned by Harold Bartram from 1922 – 1974. He cleared the weeds and ran the property as a model dairy farm and later purchased and joined it with Cleveland Estate. He also owned several hundred acres in Heidelberg, Bulleen and Templestowe.

The Bartram family operated a Dairy Machine business in Melbourne which was established in 1870, producing milk, cream, butter and cheese, including butter for export. The Bartram's lived at Heidelberg, then moved to Viewbank in 1942, building a home near Banyule Road.

Bartram sold parts of Cleveland Estate in the 1950s as large sub-divisions. Part of Viewbank and the lower section of Cleveland were sold to the State Government in the early 1980s for the Yarra Valley Parklands. The rest of Viewbank was subdivided and sold for suburban housing.

Many people are familiar with the three Viewbank silos, clearly visible from Banyule Road, opposite Apple Blossom Court. They can be seen from the Plenty River Trail but there is no pathway access to them. The site comprises structures associated with the Bartram dairy - three silage silos erected between 1931 and 1936 and a shed. There are also several flat areas with brick rubble, the likely sites of other dairy buildings.

The silos were restored by the Victorian Government in 2018, as the roof of one had blown off in a storm and they were all in poor condition. The project had some unique technical challenges, including reconstruction of the unusual dodecahedral (12 planes) roof on one of the silos.

**Community celebration of the silo restoration and re-roofing June 2018**

A detailed history of Viewbank is provided in the 1996 Viewbank Homestead Historical Survey by Sera Peters.

## Continue walking along the Trail

The Trail then passes the land leased by Riding for the Disabled, the North Eastern Pony Club and Viewbank weather station, onto Martins Lane, which is the northern boundary of Crown Land Portions 6 and 7. The Trail crosses into Crown Land Portion 7 at Hendersons Rd.

### Site 4: Melbourne Water Pipeline Reserve

The Melbourne Water Pipeline Reserve runs from the Plenty River Trail at Martins Lane across the Plenty River to the corner of Bonds and Rosehill Roads in Lower Plenty. It provides a cleared walkway down to the Plenty River.

The Reserve contains an underground Main Water Supply Pipeline from the Silvan Reservoir to Melbourne. A pressure release valve is located just inside the gates. The Pipeline Reserve is being considered as a route for a multi-purpose trail across the River to connect with Bonds Road.

## To continue the circuit walk, turn south down Seymour Road, a gravel road at the east end of Martins Lane. Alternatively, continue north on the Plenty River Trail from Martins Lane to Yallambie, referring to Section 2 notes

### Seymour Road

Seymour Road is a narrow unmade road that services several private properties that back onto the Plenty River. It joins Banyule Road on a steep cutting and bend.

**Seymour Rd, near Martins Lane**

**Henty Road Bridge**

## Turn left, onto Banyule Road and <u>carefully</u> cross to the eastern side of the Plenty River via the Henty Road Bridge

### Site 5: Henty Road-Banyule Road Bridge

This narrow bridge of steel and concrete, with bluestone abutments crosses the Plenty River and links the suburbs of Viewbank and Lower Plenty. The bridge was built in the 1920s to facilitate better access to the Cleveland Estate and properties in Bonds Road.

## Walk along Henty Road and turn right into Cleveland Avenue

### East Side of the Plenty River

The east side walk was first mapped by Russell Yeoman of Eltham District Historical Society, titled *Lower Plenty River and Red Gum Walk*. This section of the walk is based on Russell's work and his research is greatly appreciated.

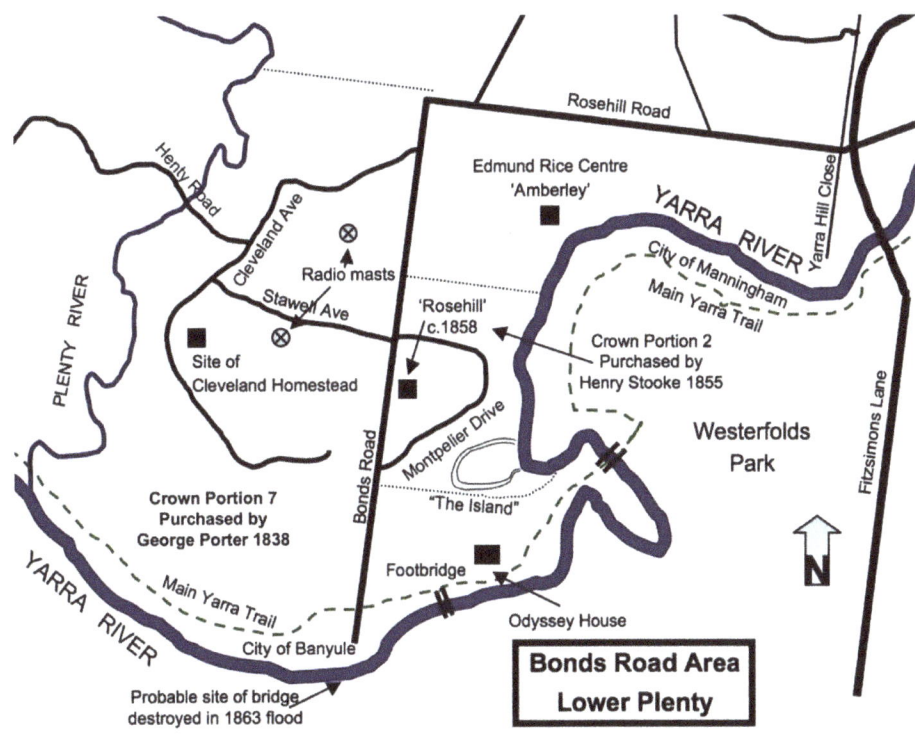

Map courtesy Russell Yeoman and Jim Connor, Eltham District Historical Society

## Crown Land Portion 7

The first European settlers in the area were squatters Edward and James Willis who arrived in April 1837. The land was surveyed as part of Crown Land Portion 7 and sold in 1838. Portion 7 extended north from the Yarra River to Martins Lane and from Hendersons Road in the west to Bonds Road in the east and contained the Plenty River. It was auctioned on 12 September 1838 and was purchased by merchant George Porter, who named it Cleveland Estate.

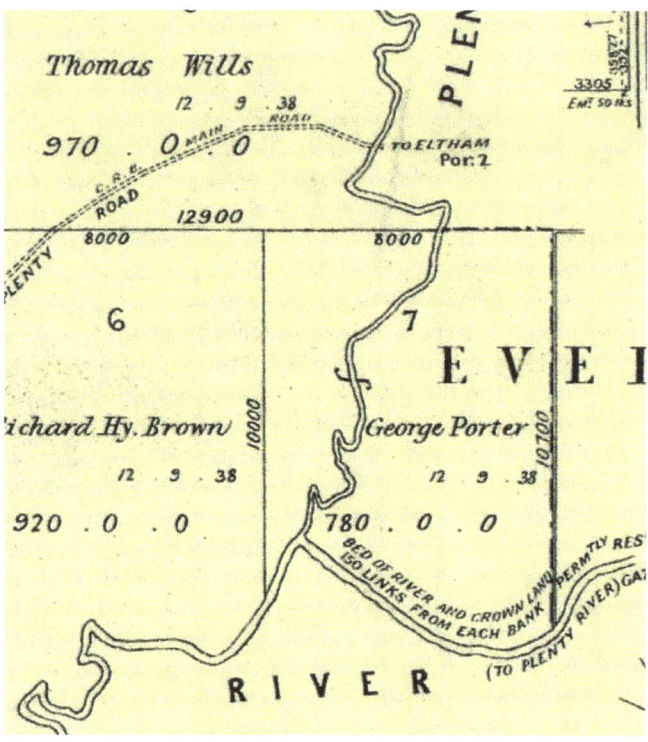

Map of Portion 7 - Parish of Keelbundora 1837. Source: State Library Victoria

## Site 6: Wanstead – the Pastoral Run of Early European Squatters Edward and James Willis

This site takes in a broad sweep of land on the eastern side of the Plenty River, bounded on the south and east by the Yarra River. The Willis brothers used the area as a sheep run from April 1837, initially crossing the Plenty River close to Yarra and setting up camp. They named their 'station' Wanstead after their parent's property in Tasmania.

The 1837 diary by James Willis details their journey from Tasmania, along with their 659 pure-bred merino sheep. The Diary spans April to August 1837 and is an important primary account of the activities of early Victorian squatters.

Arriving at Point Gellibrand (Williamstown) on 13 April 1837, they journey along the north bank of the Yarra River, and arrive at John Woods Sheep run on Tuesday 18 April (Site 1) where they get help from his shepherd Old Tom.

> "...... we procured the assistance of Old Tom the shepherd, who conducted us to a creek about two miles off running in a northerly direction. ....We crossed it and came to our present [site], which although thickly timbered we have every reason to be satisfied with. It is bounded in the South and East by the Yarra. The stream I have alluded to forms its western boundary ... which I perceive the surveyors have named the 'River Plenty', while to the north we have a forest..."
>
> (James Willis Diary, 18 April 1837.)

They built yards and cleared a ford over the Plenty River, which they called Edwards Rivulet and brought their sheep, carts and equipment over to Wanstead, with much difficulty, due to the steep river bank. They lived in tents then a wattle and daub (mud) hut on the ridge behind the present Lower Plenty Hotel, on what is now Heidelberg Golf Club land. Robert Hoddle describes the site as 'Mr Willis's sheep station – hut' in his Field Survey notes 28 July 1837.

As well as visits to Melbourne town and neighbours they explored the area and in mid July 1837

> "...... when we had traversed the course of our creek the 'Plenty' (or Edward's Rivulet, as we call it) for some five or six miles, we came upon a tract of most excellent grazing land, which Master Ned thought so much superior to his own run ....that Ned determined in his own mind to move to this desirable spot forthwith. We therefore rode to the top of a high hill, from which we enjoyed a view of the surrounding country for twenty miles or more in every direction."
>
> (James Willis Diary, 15 July 1837)

Shortly after James became very ill, blaming winter and sleeping on the ground. He was taken to Melbourne for medical care. His next diary entry is 30 August, 1837.

> "I thank God that I am at length quite restored to health.....When I returned home about a week ago, I found Ned had removed his sheep and headquarters to a far more desirable spot about seven miles higher up the 'Plenty' and for the first time we found ourselves in a snug turf hut eleven feet by thirteen, with a thatched roof and neatly whitewashed inside. Ned has a respectable bedstead in one corner built of wattle sticks, one in the opposite corner is being made for (brother) William, whose arrival we are expecting....in the corner near the chimney is a (rough) sofa by day and my bed by night."
>
> (James Willis Diary, Thursday 30 August 1837)

This new site was recorded as *'Mr Willis Hut'* by Robert Hoddle in his Field Survey notes 4 August 1837. It is located on the west side of the Plenty River, south of the current Tanundra wetlands in the Plenty Gorge Parklands, previously part of Janefield.

The Willis brothers vacated their Plenty River sheep run in 1839 after receiving a notice to quit in March 1839, due to imminent Crown Land Sales.

James and his other brother William, who part owned the sheep, acquired a 400 acre property on the Plenty River at Bridge Inn Rd, Mernda in 1840, again naming it Wanstead. James also established the first Bridge Inn Hotel on the property, which they sold in 1851. This hotel site was recently excavated by Heritage Victoria. James later served in senior administrative positions in local government and the Supreme Court. He died in South Yarra in 1873.

Edward Willis initially went back to Tasmania to attend to family matters. He returned to Victoria and moved the Wanstead sheep to his property, Koolomurt in the Western District, where he developed one of the finest merino studs in Victoria, as well as being a successful merchant and philanthropist. (Willis, E. 1883). He returned to England in 1894 and died in Reading in 1895.

## Cleveland Estate and George Porter

George Isaac Porter (1800 - 1848) and family arrived in Sydney in 1835 and established a successful merchant business. He purchased Crown Land Portion 7 on 12 September 1838. They moved to Port Phillip District with a house in Melbourne as well as at Lower Plenty, both of which he named Cleveland after his former home in Yorkshire. He also owned several other properties, including Portion 4 on the Darebin Creek.

> *"George Porter was originally in the British East India Company Army. He went on to work as overseer of Calcutta Botanical Gardens, then helped establish the Penang Botanical Gardens, along with teaching roles, before moving into the mercantile trade. In Melbourne he was a founding member of the Mechanics Institute and was active in public life."*
>
> *(Marsden, A. and Langdon, M. 2014)*

Porter was the only original purchaser in the area who retained ownership of his property. He farmed the land and likely used his botanical knowledge for its horticulture. The 1841 Census of Cleveland listed nine persons, with James Tailor in charge, and a house built of wood and stone.

After Porter's death in 1848 the Cleveland property appears to have been infrequently occupied by the Porter family, apart from a brief period of residence by his son John Porter in the 1860s. Cleveland was divided into several farms that were occupied by tenant farmers, including noted ploughman Thomas Mundy and Joseph Bond from 1855 - 96.

Crops included potatoes and hay, and Cleveland became a well established farming area. However the area was subject to floods by the Yarra, which in 1863 destroyed crops and livelihoods, with some farms being repossessed by the Porter family. The property declined and just after the turn of the century Cleveland was described in the McBriar report as being:

> *"A good example of the danger of absentee ownership ... in a filthy state with noxious weeds growing everywhere and the farmhouses and fencing in a very derelict state."*

Cleveland Estate was subdivided with some land sold in the 1920s and, as mentioned earlier, Harold Bartram buying the rest to extend his dairy farm.

> *"a local syndicate and another group bought Cleveland property after WW1 – and had a gang of men from Greensborough camped down by the Plenty River for months dealing with the noxious weeds and cleaning the place up. Only some of the land was bought before the depression, the rest was bought later by the Bartram's of Viewbank."*

> *(McBriar, M. 1985)*

## Cleveland Avenue Points of Interest

Cleveland Avenue is a No Through Road, ending at a private property. The Rosanna Golf Club owns most of the land on the west side of Cleveland Ave, south from Henty Rd. The Golf Club moved from land along the railway line, near Rosanna Station, to this purpose built 132 acre course in 1965. The Club's land straddles the Plenty River and along with the Parks Victoria land to the south, forms an open vista with sweeping views across the landscape to the Yaruk Tamboore Wetlands.

In 1967 the MMBW had a purification works on the northern side of Cleveland Avenue, backing onto the Plenty River and Heidelberg Golf Club. The plant was demolished and the land subdivided for the Cleveland Estate residential development in the mid 1990s, with 3 hectares along the Plenty River retained for the Cleveland Wetlands Reserve.

The land on the east side of Cleveland Avenue is privately owned. The 1924 land sales plan shows a homestead site, to the south of Stawell Ave intersection, but doesn't confirm if it was built by George Porter. No remains are visible.

## Cleveland Avenue – Stawell Avenue

*Turn left into Stawell Avenue, walk to Bonds Road, turn right and walk south*

Note the series of Radio Transmission Towers in the paddocks along Stawell Avenue, as well as the significant River Red Gums.

## Bonds Road

Bonds Road forms the eastern boundary of Portion 7 and the Cleveland Estate. The land on the east side of Bonds Road was sold in five allotments by the Government in 1855, as Section 1A of the Parish of Nillumbik. Allotment 2 comprising 80 acres was purchased by Henry Stooke.

## Site 7: Rosehill Homestead

Henry Stooke built Rosehill Homestead in c.1858. It is listed on the Victorian Heritage Register as

> *"a substantial homestead of brick and locally quarried stone. It was the home of Henry Stooke, farmer, district pioneer and Chairman of the Eltham Road District, and his family and descendants until the turn of the century. It was one of the first permanent houses in the Lower Plenty area, the oldest significant homestead in the district."*

Early in the 20th Century the Bond family purchased Rosehill from Stooke's descendants and owned the property until 1958. They also bought up all the land between Rosehill Road and the Yarra River.

The Stooke Rosehill property was subdivided into residential lots in the 1960s forming Montpelier Drive. Rosehill Homestead is contained on one of the lots. It is privately owned and can be seen from the road.

**Rosehill Homestead, Bonds Road**

By the late 1970s the Catholic Church owned much of the land to the north and south of the Rosehill property.

## Amberley – Edmund Rice Centre

The Amberley property is situated to the north, off Bonds Road, via Amberley Way. The residence 'Amberley' was originally built in 1929-30 for Oswald Wallwyn Darch, and is situated on the escarpment above the Yarra River. In the late 1970s it was extended and operated as a Christian Brothers Training Centre. The complex, now known as the Edmund Rice Centre, operates as a school camp, retreat, conference and function centre.

Most of the Amberley land was subdivided for residential development in the early 1990s.

## Site 8: Seminary of the Blessed Sacrament Fathers - Odyssey House

At the southern end of Bonds Road, the Seminary of the Blessed Sacrament Fathers was built in the 1950s. It can be seen from Bonds Road and now houses Odyssey House, an Alcohol and other Drugs Residential Rehabilitation Community. Most of the former seminary land was included in the Yarra Valley Parklands.

The suspension bridge behind the Seminary was built to enable Priests to have easier access to Melbourne and for residents of Templestowe to attend services. The bridge is well worth the short side trip east along the Main Yarra Trail, with platypuses sometimes visible in the shallows at dusk.

**Odyssey House, from Bonds Road, with Montpelier Reserve in the foreground**

## Continue walking south down Bonds Road to the Main Yarra Trail

### Bonds Road - Southern End

Bonds Road is a dead end road finishing just before the Yarra River. It intersects with the Main Yarra Trail and is a popular car parking area for Main Yarra Trail users. The old roadway continues a short distance toward the Yarra, but there is no access to the River. The area is very overgrown, slippery and intersected by unofficial mountain bike trails.

The 1945 Melbourne Aerial survey map shows there were farm houses on both sides, near the end of Bonds Road, though little remains. Two large old stone pillars mark a driveway entrance as a feature on the eastern side at the end of Bonds Road, along with fencing, remnant fruit trees and compacted earth of a likely dwelling site.

**Pillars of driveway entrance off Bonds Road**

**Old roadway at end of Bonds Road**

A punt operated across the Yarra in the area in the 1850s, with a wooden bridge built in 1855 to transport produce. It connected Bonds Road to Thompsons Road - Templestowe Road, linking the communities and shortening the journey to Eltham.

The bridge was badly damaged by the Yarra flood of 1863 but requests to government to fund a replacement were unsuccessful. The bridge was repaired in 1873 and almost washed away in the October 1923 flood, when it was described as, *"a solid wooden structure on an iron girder, with stone supports."*

The bridge also survived the December 1934 flood and was in use until about 1935, when it was declared unsafe and abandoned, with its remnants washed away in the 1960s. The overhead powerlines follow the alignment of the bridge. (Padula, B. 2020)

Bridge, Templestowe Road, near Heidelberg - 14 May 1899
Photo by Daniel, Mark. Source: State Library Victoria

## Site 9: Restoring our environmental heritage – Murundaka Grasslands and Swamp, the Yaruk Tamboore Wetlands and the Montpelier Grasslands, Billabong and Swamp

The crescent of open land south of Cleveland Avenue, from the lower eastern boundary of Rosanna Golf Course, across Bonds Road to the western side of the Yarra forms part of the Yarra Valley Parklands.

The land west of Bonds Road forms the Murundaka (Stay, live at) Grasslands with the Murundaka Swamp near the Main Yarra Trail, immediately west of Bonds Road. The Yaruk Tamboore (Magical Pool) Wetlands are further along the Trail near the boundary of Rosanna Golf Course. These two site names were decided by the Wurundjeri Council in 2010.

The Montpelier Grasslands, Billabong and Island are on the eastern side of Bonds Road.

Murundaka and Montpelier comprise a substantial area of Ecological Vegetation Classes of Plains Grassy Woodland and Plains Grassy Wetland.

Major environmental restoration of the Murundaka area has been undertaken over the last decade, as a collaboration led by the Friends of Yarra Valley Parks, together with Parks Victoria, Melbourne Water, Rosanna Golf Course and Banyule Council. The land was overrun with weeds, rabbits and foxes.

Previous land use included orchards, cattle grazing and a dairy farm established by the Cock family. It was sold to the Board of Works in the 1980s for the Yarra Valley Parklands.

Before reservoirs changed the Yarra's natural flows the area would have been fed by seasonal floods, giving the River Red Gums the soaking needed to survive droughts and triggering the breeding of fish, crustaceans and birds. A small creek fed the wetland, running from east to west before joining the Plenty River. When Rosanna Golf Course was built the creek's western section was filled in, with its flow diverted via a drain on the boundary of the golf course, into the Yarra River.

### Re-flooding of Yaruk Tamboore Wetlands and Murundaka Swamp

With funding from Melbourne Water, the Friends of Yarra Valley Parks have rehabilitated the area to enable the wetlands to hold water all year around. They installed wetland sills to restrict water loss, dug several large ponds and used a draught horse to manoeuvre red gum logs into the pools, to provide habitat for fish and yabbies and perches for birds. This was followed by extensive plantings.

At the initiative of the Friends of Yarra Valley Parks, Melbourne Water has also undertaken a $400,000 project to rehabilitate Montpelier Billabong, along with the control of pest species.

The Murundaka area is best appreciated from the Main Yarra Trail or by looking south from behind the Rosanna Golf Club car park in Cleveland Avenue. Access is limited as it is a conservation area and some of the land is also leased for cattle grazing. The Montpelier area can be seen from Bonds Road, between Montpelier Drive and Odyssey House.

Andrew Lucas FOYVP with Ben the Suffolk draught horse moving logs into Murundaka Swamp - Yaruk Tamboore Wetlands Photo: Andrew Lucas

## *Turn right onto the Main Yarra Trail and walk back toward Somerset Drive to complete the circuit*

### Site 10: Yan-Yan, the confluence of Yarra and Plenty Rivers

The Yarra and Plenty confluence is a peaceful spot, with a simple raised pedestrian / cyclist bridge. Note: there is no access from Cleveland Avenue or Rosanna Golf Course. Remnant European plantings are scattered throughout the landscape but the sense of place lies in the indigenous heritage, vegetation and birdlife. A bench seat is conveniently located to the side of the bridge.

**Plenty River and pedestrian bridge, just above the confluence with Birrarung**

Robert Hoddle located his Survey Camp on the west side of the Plenty River, near the south western end of Rosanna Golf Club on 26 July 1837.

### Site 11: Banyule Billabong

The Banyule Billabong is located alongside the Yarra, near the Plenty River Trail turnoff. It holds cultural connection for the Wurundjeri people, as well as being a popular recreation site and home to many plant and animal species. The Billabong was recharged with 51.3 mega litres of environmental water, pumped from the Yarra River in 2019 by Melbourne Water and Banyule Council in partnership with the Victorian Environmental Water Holder, the Wurundjeri Council and Parks Victoria.

The Billabong quickly came back to life with frogs and birds.

The Banyule Swamp, just past the Somerset Avenue car park, below Banyule House is worth a side trip and is another fine example of successful environmental rehabilitation by the community.

## *The walk concludes back at the Somerset Ave car park*

Banyule Billabong being recharged in 2019.

Banyule Billabong 2020
Photos: Sarah Gaskill

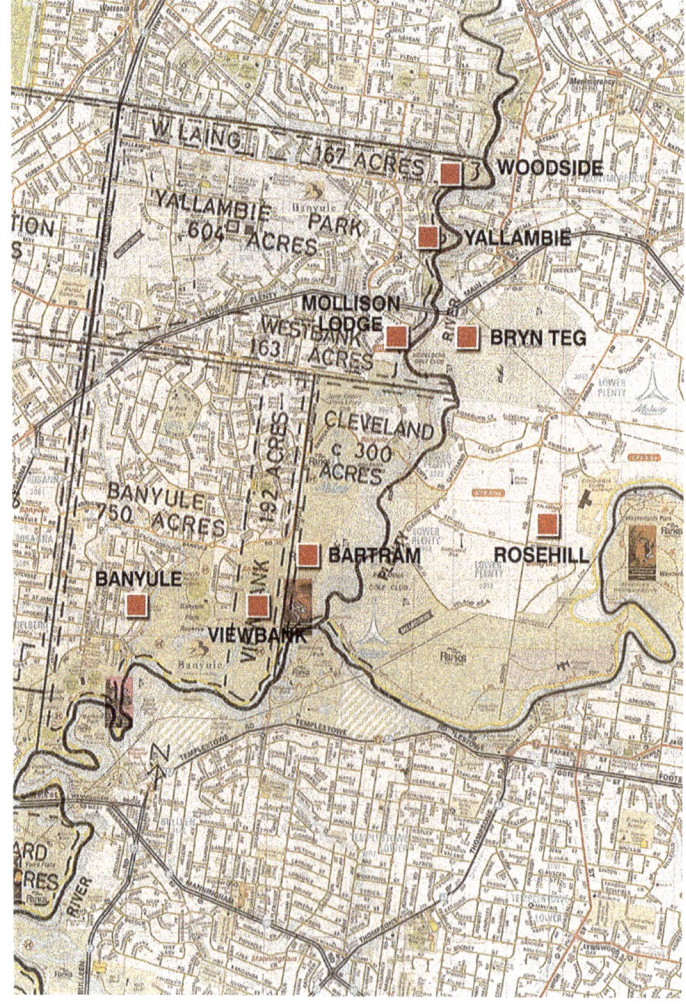

Homesteads near the Yarra and Lower Plenty River - Map by Ian McLachlan, 1999

Andrew Lucas FOYVP with Ben the Suffolk draught horse moving logs into Murundaka Swamp - Yaruk Tamboore Wetlands. Photo courtesy Andrew Lucas

Start of the Plenty River Trail, on the Main Yarra Trail, Viewbank

# References

Bolderwood, Rolf. 1896. *Old Melbourne Memories* MacMillan https://en.wikisource.org/wiki/Old_Melbourne_Memories

Bryant, Ian. 2022. *Robert Hoddle 1837 Field Survey Notes*, unpublished research

Garden, D. 1972. *Heidelberg the Land and its People 1838-1900*. Melbourne University Press

Hayes, S. 2014. *Good Taste, Fashion, Luxury: A Genteel Melbourne Family and their Rubbish*. Studies in Australasian Historical Archaeology Volume 5 https://open.sydneyuniversitypress.com.au/9781743324172.html

Lucas, A and Edington, C. *Murundaka and Montpelier Precinct*. Murundaka Rehabilitation Project, Lower Plenty.

Marsden, Anne and Langdon, Marcus. 2014. *George Isaac Porter: Across two worlds* in June 2014 edition of the Victorian Historical Journal of the Royal Historical Society of Victoria

McBriar, M. and Loder and Bayly, 1985. *Heidelberg Conservation Study Part 2, Historical Riverland Landscape Assessment, Maps A – D*

McLachlan, Ian. 1999, Map of Homesteads near the Yarra River and Lower Plenty River.

Meadows, J. and Lindsay. B. 2017. *Re-Imagining Birrarung*. Environment Justice Australia

Padula, B. 2020 *Tracks, Trails and Coasts Near Melbourne*. Online

Peters, Sera. 1996. *Viewbank Homestead, Heidelberg. A Historical Survey*. Heritage Victoria

Poulter, Jim. 2020. *What Treaty? Examining Batman's 1835 Port Phillip Excursion from an Aboriginal Perspective,* Melbourne

Report of the Select Committee of the Legislative Council on Aborigines 1858-1859 https://aiatsis.gov.au/sites/default/files/docs/digitised_collections/remove/92768.pdf

Weaver, Fiona. 1991, *Lower Plenty Archaeological Survey*, MMBW. Melbourne

Willis, Edward. 1883 *Koolomurt Stud Flocks*, in Camperdown Chronicle 10 October 1883, p2

Willis, James. 1837 *A Pioneer Squatters Life* in Historical Records of Victoria. Vol 6, Chapter 8

Wurundjeri Cultural Heritage website https://www.wurundjeri.com.au/

# Footprints on the Landscape:

## The Willis Family, Wanstead and the Plenty River 1837 – 1851

The Willis brothers were early squatters, then settlers on the Plenty River. Their story is a cameo of colonisation in Victoria and the development of our wool industry. These edited notes were originally prepared for a 2018 Parks Victoria / Melbourne Water community walk.

| Date | Event | Details |
|---|---|---|
| 1823 | Willis family and 100 Spanish merino sheep arrive in Van Diemen's Land - establish Wanstead Park in Central Tasmania | **WANSTEAD PARK Van Diemen's Land (Tasmania)**<br><br>Richard Willis b. 1777 Kirkswald Cumberland, shoemaker London. Married Anne Harper b. 1780 St.Kitts. They Migrated to Van Diemen's Land with 11 children.<br><br>Arrived Hobart Town on ship 'Courier' 2 December 1823. Brought out 100 sheep of Spanish Merino pedigree, bred from stock given to King George of England by the King of Spain in 1809. Granted 3000 acres near Campbell Town. Named his estate 'Wanstead' after a village in Essex. Completed building grand house of Pise (rammed earth) in 1828. |
| 1837 | James, Edward & uncle Arthur and 659 sheep set sail for Port Phillip | Richard Willis is harsh and authoritarian toward his family and quarrelsome with neighbours and business associates, but remained on good terms with Lieutenant-Governor Sir George Arthur who appointed him a MLC.<br><br>His son James Louis (1814 - 1873) worked as a clerk in Hobart. Edward (1816 - 1895) managed the Wanstead farm. These two brothers and their Uncle Arthur leave Van Diemen's Land with 659 sheep and sail for Port Phillip on 9 April 1837. The sheep were bred from their fathers Wanstead stock and are jointly owned by Willis brothers Edward, Charles and William. |
| 9 April 1837 | James Louis Willis commences his diary on departure from Georgetown Tasmania | **James Willis Diary – A Pioneer Squatters Life 1837**<br><br>James Louis Willis commences his diary which details their journey from Tasmania, and squatting on the Plenty River at Lower Plenty with their sheep. |

|  |  |  |
|---|---|---|
|  |  | The Diary forms Chapter 8 of the Historical Records of Victoria, Volume 6. It is the earliest known primary record of European settlement in Lower Plenty, presenting a short but significant record of the exploits of the Willis brothers and the many challenges they faced. It is set against the backdrop of early Melbourne town and European colonisation of Victoria. |
|  |  | The Diary also reveals a troubled Willis family and sons driven from home by an unforgiving father, for an apparently contrived offence and episodes of *'tyrannical, brutal conduct'* toward his wife and children. These family dynamics provide a sad context of why two educated young men and their Uncle have embarked on this venture, not as brazen speculators seeking land and wealth, which characterised many of Victoria's early European inhabitants. |
|  |  | The first Diary entry on 9 April 1837 describes sailing from Georgetown, on the ship *Siren*. It goes on to detail their journey to Lower Plenty, their labours in establishing their sheep run, their daily survival activities in living off the land and the challenges of camp life. It describes the landscape and weather and includes details of their exploration of the Plenty River, trips into Melbourne town with associated events and visits to neighbours. |
|  |  | It also reveals the hopes and aspirations of a lonely young man, driven away from family and friends and his concern for his mother and siblings, due to the unpredictable behaviour of his father. |
|  |  | Early in the diary James identifies himself as best suited to be a 'quill driver', as he doesn't own any of the sheep. In later life he successfully holds senior administrative positions in Victoria. |
| 13 April 1837 | Arrival - Port Phillip District | **Key Diary Entries** The Willis Brothers arrive at Point Gellibrand (Williamstown) and their shepherds carry the sheep ashore. |
| 16 - 22 April 1837 | James & Edward journey to Lower Plenty – cross the Plenty River and establish their sheep run, naming it Wanstead | **WANSTEAD Plenty River at Lower Plenty** The brother's journey with their sheep, shepherds, wagon and horses along northern side of the Yarra River, cross the Plenty River, and establish a camp on land bounded on the South and East by Yarra and west by Plenty River and squat there until July. The location is identified by Robert Hoddle in his field survey notes 28 July 1837. |

| | | |
|---|---|---|
| | | They name their sheep run Wanstead, built stock yards, dig a ford to move their sheep and equipment across the Plenty River, and work as *'common labourers'*. They are in dread of losing their sheep to attack by the *'wild dogs of the country'*, and at night are *'regaled by their hideous howls'* |
| May - July 1837 | Settling into life on the Plenty River | Entries detail the daily activities of his *'monotonous life'*, local bird life, letter writing to family, visits to Melbourne, visitors and visits to neighbours and exploration of the area. Uncle Arthur returns to Tasmania, finding squatter life too hard with the onset of winter. |
| 15 July 1837 | Exploring the Plenty River | **James & Edward (Ned) explore the Plenty River**<br><br>In mid-July they travel upstream and *"when we had traversed the course of our creek the 'Plenty' (or Edward's Rivulet, as we call it) for some five or six miles, we came upon a tract of most excellent grazing land, which Master Ned (Edward) thought so much superior to his own run ….that Ned determined in his own mind to move to this desirable spot forthwith. We therefore rode to the top of a high hill, from which we enjoyed a view of the surrounding country for twenty miles or more in every direction."*<br>(James Willis Diary, Saturday 15 July 1837) |
| 30 Aug 1837 | Final diary entry by James Willis – a new camp on the Plenty River | **Final Diary Entry: New Camp site - Plenty River, Janefield**<br><br>The Diary ends on 30 August, with a lengthy entry after a gap of 6 weeks. James has returned to the Plenty River after recovering from serious illness in Melbourne Town. Edward has moved camp to a new site upstream on the Plenty River.<br><br>*"I thank God that I am at length quite restored to health…..When I returned home about a week ago, I found Ned had removed his sheep and headquarters to a far more desirable spot about seven miles higher up the 'Plenty' and for the first time we found ourselves in a snug turf hut eleven feet by thirteen, with a thatched roof and neatly whitewashed inside. Ned has a respectable bedstead in one corner built of wattle sticks, one in the opposite corner is being made for (brother) William, whose arrival we are expecting….in the corner near the chimney is a (rough) sofa by day and my bed by night."*<br>(James Willis Diary, Thursday 30 August 1837) |

|  |  | The location is identified by Robert Hoddle in his survey notes 4 August 1837, on west side of Plenty River, south of current day Tanunda Wetlands. |
|---|---|---|
|  |  | In this final entry James is looking forward to moving to Geelong to be in charge of a mercantile firm named Willis, Garrett & Co while also reflecting on his family and life as a *'banished person.'* |
|  |  | After being drawn into the lives of two young men this last entry leaves a desire to know what happened to the brothers Willis. Further research has revealed how their lives played out and their considerable contribution to Victoria's development. |
| **Feb 1839** | Willis parents return to England | Richard & Anne Willis return England, leaving their 5 sons in the colonies. They had 18 children, with 10 alive in 1836. Richard Willis died at Southsea in 1855. |
| **24 March 1839** | Edward quits his camp as land sales imminent | Land sales commence on the west side of the Plenty River in 1838 and bring an end to the brief squatting era in the Lower Plenty. Edward Willis, in a letter dated 24 March 1839 states he was leaving the Plenty River *"having notice to quit due to the imminent land sales."* |
| **Late 1839 - 1843** | Edward returns to Van Diemen's Land Wanstead, marries, then returns to Victoria | Edward returns to Van Diemen's Land in 1839. He marries Catherine Swanston, 12 September 1840, daughter of Captain Charles Swanston a leading member of the Port Phillip Association. Edward is listed in the 1842 and 1843 census as Person in Charge of Wanstead, with Richard Willis as Proprietor.<br><br>Edward returns to Victoria in 1843 and in partnership with Capt Swanston becomes a respected merino breeder in the Western District at Koolomurt, a prosperous trader, philanthropist and resident of Geelong. |
| **1840** | James & William lease or buy 400 acres & hut in Mernda | **Portion 19, Parish of Morang**<br><br>This land was acquired by Arthur Sergeantson in February 1840. He erected the Carome Mill in the southern part of Portion 19 in 1841. The northern part was leased or sold to James Willis and his younger brother William in 1840. They again named it Wanstead and likely moved their sheep there from Janefield as William (b. 1817) was a part owner of the sheep and Edward was in Van Diemen's Land. |

| | | |
|---|---|---|
| 1840 | Establish Bridge Inn Hotel, name the property Wanstead | **WANSTEAD – Bridge Inn Plenty River Mernda**<br><br>JW Payne, (1975) states that *"when the Willis brothers James and Lewis took up 'Wanstead' on the Plenty River in 1840 they lost little time in converting to an Inn a wattle and daub house which stood beside the stream ... by 1841 it bore the title of The Bridge Inn, with James and Lewis Willis as licensee, to supplement their income from 'Wanstead' their pastoral lease."* (Note: Lewis is a transcribing error of James's middle name Louis, along with omission of William, from the 1841 Census.) |
| 1841 | 1841 Census – James Louis & William Willis own Wanstead | **WANSTEAD - 1841 Census Return Number 66**<br><br>Surname: WILLIS First Name: William and James Louis.<br><br>Owner's Surname: WILLIS. Owner's First Names: William and James Louis. Residence: Wanstead, River Plenty, County Burke, District Port Phillip. |
| April 20 1841 | Licensee Bridge Inn - James Louis Willis | **Bridge Inn Hotel River Plenty Mernda**<br><br>Publicans Licences April 20 1841 - New Licences in the Country: RIVER PLENTY James Louis Willis - "Bridge Inn" |
| April 1851 | James & William sell Mernda Wanstead to Moses Thomas | **Mernda Wanstead sold**<br><br>In 1851 James & William Willis sold their Mernda Wanstead pastoral holding with 400 acres and the Bridge Inn to Moses Thomas. It was named Marsh Farm, then Mayfield. |
| 1850 - 1873 | James Willis's career | James Louis Willis was elected Geelong's First Treasurer 1850 - 1851 and resided at Hearne Hill, Geelong. He was then appointed Clerk of Petty Sessions in Kyneton - Woodend and Commissioner of the Supreme Court of Melbourne in 1871. He died at his home - Avoca Cottage, Punt Road, South Yarra on 28 April 1873 aged 58 years, survived by his three daughters. |

| 10 Oct 1883 | Edward Willis confirms Koolomurt merinos are bred from stock brought to Van Diemen's Land by his father in 1823 | **WANSTEAD SHEEP**<br><br>At some stage after Edward returned to Victoria the Lower Plenty - Janefield - Mernda Wanstead sheep were relocated to Koolomurt, possibly by William Willis. The relocation is confirmed in an article written by Edward Willis in the Camperdown Chronicle 10 October 1883. He talks about his noted flocks and a ram which has recently won champion prize at the Coleraine show.<br><br>Edward writes: *"These flocks are of the purest Spanish merino blood from time immemorial. They were formerly the joint property of Messrs. Edward and William Willis and Mr. C. L. Swanston. In 1809, the King of Spain presented to his late Majesty, George the Third, 2000 merino sheep; they were Cavana Paular, one of the finest in point of pile, and esteemed for beauty of carcass.*<br><br>*In 1824, my father, the late Richard Willis, M.L.C. of Wanstead Park, purchased from his late Majesty, George the Third, 50 young ewes and three lambs, selected from the above, and imported them to Tasmania, where they were bred separately with great care as to selection. In 1837, my father presented my late brother (William) and myself with a fine selection of five hundred (500) young ewes and rams from his pure flocks. These sheep I imported into Victoria in the month of April of that year."*<br><br>Edward discusses his selective breeding program at Koolomurt, to increase the density of their wool and that *"... the whole stock of Koolomurt breeding ewes, consisting of eight or ten thousand are of this pure breed."* This article confirms the contribution to the development of Victoria's merino wool industry by the Willis brothers, from humble beginnings on the Plenty River, to large flocks at Koolomurt in the Western District.<br><br>In 1894 Edward returned to England and lived on his property, Seven Oaks, in Kent. He died at Goring near Reading on 9 August 1895, predeceased by his wife and survived by two sons and three daughters. Other than Edwards reference to William as deceased in the above article, his activities after Mernda are unknown.<br><br>Koolomurt currently operates as a sheep and beef farm. Further research is needed to establish the fate of the Willis sheep. |

| 1927 | Reminiscences of the Plenty River by Walter Thomas in 1927  | Childhood memories of the Plenty River by Walter Thomas, complete the story and provide important insight. He was the son of Moses Thomas, who bought the Wanstead - Bridge Inn property from James and William Willis in 1851.<br><br>*"After a rest we travelled to the property my late father had purchased, and on which there was a wattle and daub house that was doing duty as The Bridge Inn, although there was no bridge near the place. We arrived about 4pm in April, 1851...The Plenty River then was a beautiful stream of water, clear as crystal, fish swimming about and with a strong flow of water - very different from the present depleted stream.*<br><br>*Whilst recognising the requirements of Melbourne for an ample supply of water, I cannot in my mind help contrasting the lovely Plenty River, with its clear pellucid waters, its banks fringed with beautiful ti-tree and dogwood, and its present bare banks and small flow of often very dirty water. What has been Melbourne's gain has certainly detracted somewhat from one of God's own beautiful nature spot."*<br><br>Walter Thomas Hurstbridge Advertiser, 11 November 1927 |

# Walking the Kurrum Yallock (Plenty River)

## History, Heritage and Environment

# Section 2:
# Martins Lane to Yallambie

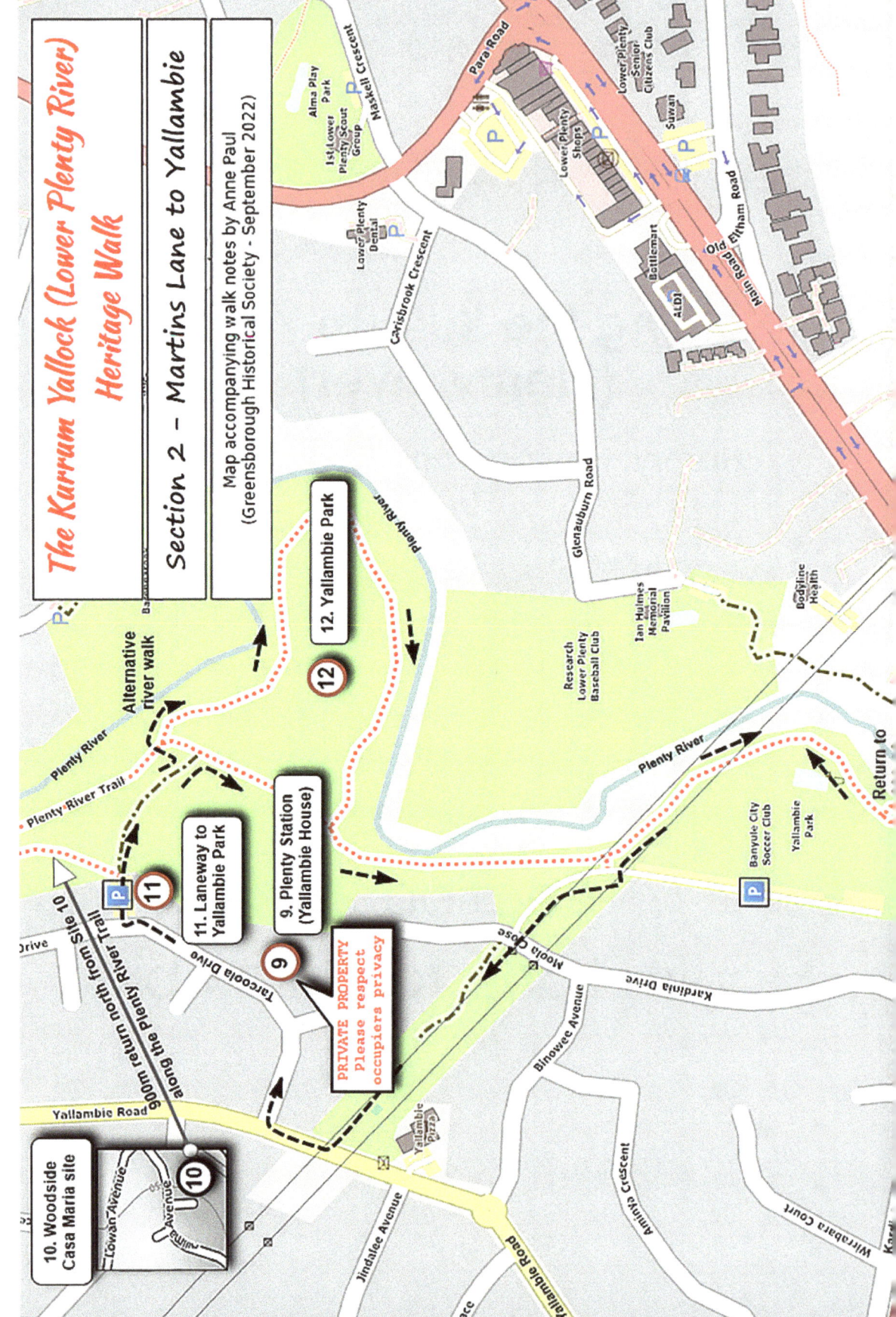

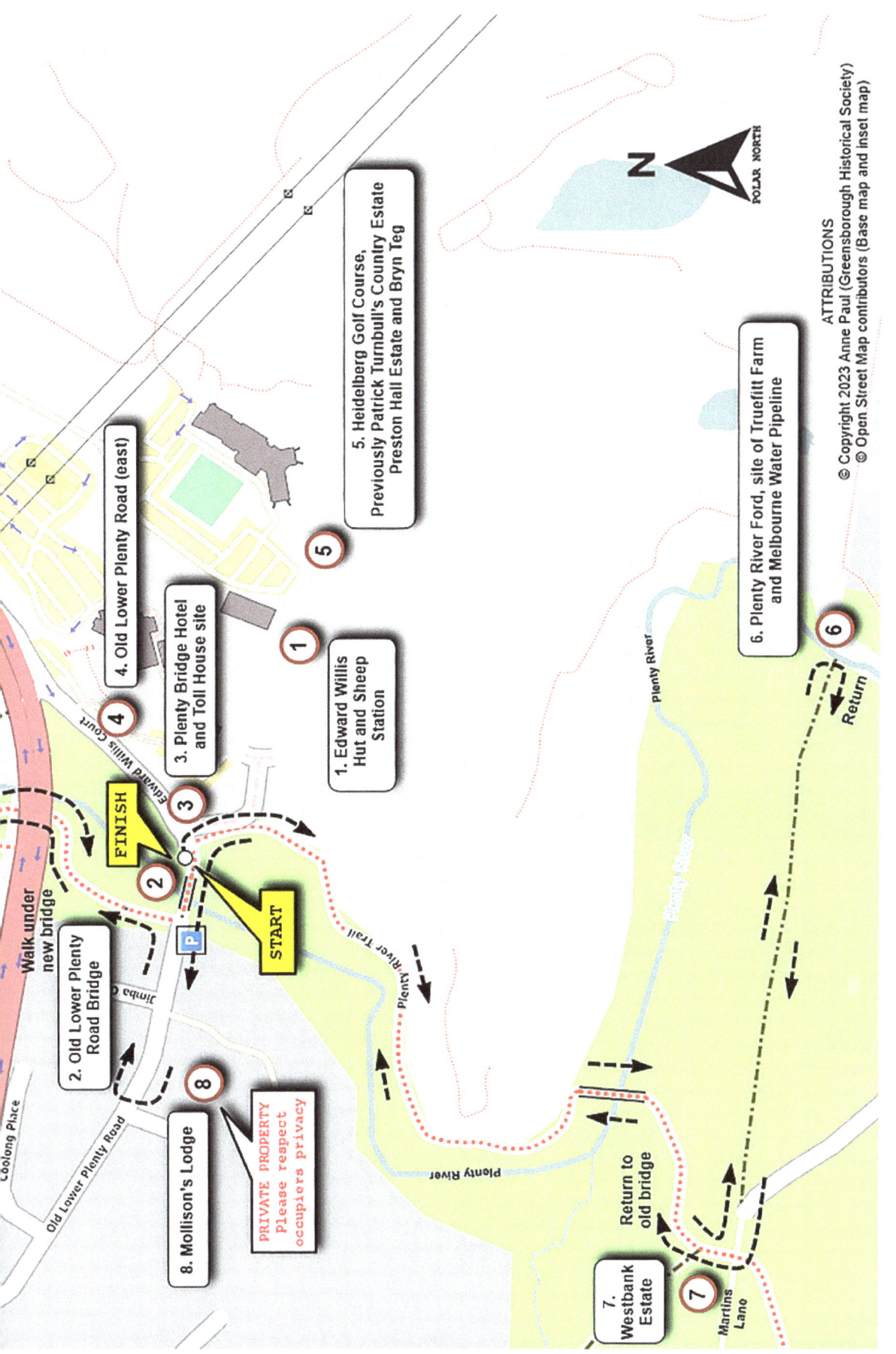

# Martins Lane to Yallambie

Kurrum Yallock, the Plenty River has a rich and complex heritage, including its early European settlement. Some sites remain, often merged into the landscape, while others are preserved only in photos or oral history.

This walk starts at the Old Lower Plenty Road Bridge, on the Plenty River Trail and links in with the Section 1 walk. It explores the history of some of the main sites in the Yallambie - Lower Plenty area, via a figure of eight loop taking approximately 2 - 3 hours.

**Pre-European Settlement**

The Plenty River and Valley is part of the territory of the Wurundjeri-willam, a clan of the Kulin Nation of central Victoria. Their territory extends across the Birrarung (Yarra River) Valley and its tributaries.

There was a substantial campsite in Yallambie Park, where the long deep pool provided good fishing. Scar trees near Seymour Road and in Rosanna Golf Course, along with several artifact scatters, were identified in the 1991 archaeological survey along the Plenty River. (Weaver, F. 1991)

The confluence of the Yarra and Plenty Rivers was noted as a ceremonial site by the Assistant Protector of Aborigines, William Thomas, in the Report of the Select Committee of the Legislative Council on the Aborigines, 1859.

There is some remnant pre-European vegetation, notably the ancient River Red Gum, on private land east of Old Lower Plenty Bridge, with several specimens in Heidelberg Golf Course, as well as further downstream. The majority of vegetation was cleared for agricultural purposes, leaving only a narrow riparian strip along the river bank and some shade trees.

**European Settlement along the Plenty River**

The Lower Plenty was one of the earliest settled areas in Port Phillip District. In his 1836 journal Joseph Gellibrand, pastoralist and explorer notes he came upon *"fine feeding land … and a rapid stream of water"* which he called the Plenty River.

Squatters first occupied the area in the mid 1830s, with the land surveyed into Crown Land Portions by Robert Hoddle and his survey team in 1837. The first rural land sales in Port Phillip District were for the Lower Plenty region, being held in Sydney on 12 September 1838. Portions 7 and 8 cover the Yallambie - Lower Plenty area, along and across the Plenty River.

Lower Plenty became a popular 'crossing place' providing access to settlements including Eltham, Kangaroo Ground and Yarra Flats (Yarra Glen) as it avoided the need to cross the Yarra.

The first route was approximately along Martins Lane, (50 links wide occupation road) fording the Plenty River at the bend, then round the hill and on to Eltham.

A slab hut hotel was built near this Ford. The building of the bridge further upstream shortened the route and later the Toll House and Plenty Bridge Hotel were erected nearby. Lower Plenty remained a relatively isolated rural community into the early 20th century. Subdivision of the large estates into residential and small farms around Main Road in the 1920s resulted in some housing construction, but the area remained largely semi-rural well into the 20th century, with the notable homes being Yallambie House, Bryn Teg, Preston Hall, Woodside and Mollisons Lodge.

# The Walk and Heritage Sites

The Old Lower Plenty Road Bridge area contains four heritage sites, all listed with Heritage Victoria. However housing development on land previously part of Heidelberg Golf Club has impacted this area and compromised the integrity of the Plenty River Wildlife Corridor.

### Site 1: Edward Willis Hut and Sheep Station

In April 1837 Edward Willis and brother James squatted on the eastern side of the Plenty River, near the confluence with the Yarra. They had sailed from Van Diemen's Land with 659 merino sheep, carried them ashore at Point Gellibrand (Williamstown) and herded them along the bank of the Yarra, fording the Plenty River and setting up camp. Details of their activities were recorded by James Willis in his Diary, reproduced in the Historical Records of Victoria. (Willis, J. 1837)

They named their 'sheep station' Wanstead, after their father's Tasmanian property. Thomas Walker, a significant figure in the districts early development, visited the Willis brothers and wrote that their camp was:

> "a nice situation in the fork formed by the junction of the creek Plenty and the Yarra Yarra."

The Willis sheep run extended north from the Yarra River, along the eastern side of the Plenty River, and likely past Main Road. They built stock yards and lived in tents then a wattle and daub (mud) hut on the ridge behind the Lower Plenty Hotel, on Heidelberg Golf Club land. Robert Hoddle describes the site as *'Mr Willis's sheep station – hut'* in his Field Survey notes 28 July 1837.

The 1841 census lists a wattle and daub hut and 10 inhabitants at this site. The Heidelberg Riverland Landscape Assessment Map A shows the location of the hut, east of Old Lower Plenty Road Bridge. (McBriar, M. 1985)

**Looking east into the Willis Wanstead site from Old Lower Plenty Road Bridge 2005**

## Site 2: Old Lower Plenty Road Bridge

The original Government land surveys made no provision for roads. Robert Hoddle identified a bridge in his 28 July 1837 Field Survey Notes, located on the bend, half way between Old Lower Plenty Road and Martins Lane. A ford was established downstream in 1838, at the end of Martins Lane.

In 1840 the Government proclaimed a road passing through land following the line of Old Lower Plenty Road. It crossed the River at the site of the old Bridge and was proclaimed trafficable in 1847, though residents complained in writing to authorities in 1849 as there was no bridge.

The Plenty River bridge, noted by Hoddle, or a later 1842 construction nearby was described by Richard Howitt when visiting Plenty Station in 1845 (now Yallambie).

> *"Over the Plenty is a bridge that a painter would not overlook... being picturesquely formed of trees laid across, covered with poles athwart again, and lastly overlaid with large sheets of stringy bark."*
>
> (Howitt, R. 1845)

Kangaroo Ground school teacher Andrew Ross described a bridge in 1851.

> *"At the Lower Plenty a temporary log bridge had been erected, doomed to be swept away in the approaching winter. Across the river the road lay up the hill by the fence on Turnbull's section to the top, about half a mile, where it ended, and the track had to be followed through the bush."*
>
> (Woiwod, M. 2011)

The current bluestone and iron bridge was opened on 8 March 1867. It was built by E. Chambers and Co. (iron work) and R. Turnbull (masonry) on the site of an 1858 wooden bridge. Its unique construction comprises riveted iron trusses with crossed webbing and iron plate beams to support the deck, between bluestone piers and walls on each side of the River. (Argus, 1867)

The old Bridge carried traffic for 100 years and was replaced in 1966 for safety reasons. The bend in the River to the immediate north was removed to accommodate the new bridge and Main Road alignment. The old Bridge was restored and reopened in 2001 and now forms part of the Plenty River Trail.

**Old Lower Plenty Road Bridge with Plenty River in flood**

### Site 3: Plenty Bridge Hotel and Toll House site

The Plenty Bridge Hotel was built in 1858, on the east side of the River, beside Old Lower Plenty Road. It replaced a slab hut hotel near the Martins Lane ford.

The Hotel was a staging post and resting place for drovers and miners going to the Caledonia (St Andrews) gold fields, as well as locals and served as the Post Office until the early 1920s. The 1920s Gangster Squizzy Taylor and gang were said to have stopped there on their way to their hideout near Kinglake and used an old tree across the River for target practice.

The Hotel was renamed the Golf Club Hotel in 1927 when it was purchased by the Heidelberg Golf Club. It served as the Clubs 19th hole until 1936 when a liquor license was secured by the Club. The Hotel was damaged by fire in 1950s then demolished. The Lower Plenty Hotel was later built up the hill on its current site.

Heidelberg School artist Walter Withers captures the Plenty Bridge Hotel, road and riverbank in his 1907 painting *Spring on the Lower Plenty Road, Heidelberg*. Note the two poplar trees at centre right which are consistent with photos of the Hotel.

**Spring on the Lower Plenty Road, Heidelberg, 1907, by Walter Withers.
National Gallery of Victoria**

The Toll House was on the eastern bank between the Bridge and Hotel. The Toll House was later moved to Eltham but details are unclear. In May 1879, the Argus newspaper reported a court case where two lads, Corkhill and Hodgson

> *"broke the windows of the old tollhouse, Lower Plenty bridge, some 19 years after it was built."*

## Site 4: Old Lower Plenty Road (east)

The remnant roadway was identified in Weaver's 1991 archaeological survey as a bluestone pitcher fringed road that may have led up to Bryn Teg homestead. Bitumen was laid on the road after the restoration of the old Bridge and it is likely the bluestone was removed. The Road has been recently reconstructed to provide access to the housing development. Some of the bluestone pitchers can still been seen in the front car park of the Lower Plenty Hotel. (Weaver, F. 1991)

**Plenty Bridge Hotel, Bridge and Road 1905 and 1950s**

## *Walking south along the Plenty River Trail we pass between the Plenty River and Heidelberg Golf Club*

**Site 5: Heidelberg Golf Course - Previously Patrick Turnbull's Country Estate, Preston Hall Estate and Bryn Teg**

The land that forms the Heidelberg Golf Course was part of the site of the Willis Brothers 1837 Wanstead sheep station. Its southern boundary joins Crown Land Portion 7, the Cleveland Estate.

The land was surveyed as Crown Land Portion 11, Parish of Nillumbik. It was one of the first Crown Land Sales in Nillumbik and was purchased by land speculator Captain Benjamin Baxter in 1840. Its western boundary was the Plenty River and it comprised 950 acres. (Yeoman, R. 2013)

Baxter did not develop the land which he sold to Patrick Turnbull in 1841. Turnbull was a Melbourne wine and spirit merchant and pastoralist. He cleared, fenced and stocked the land and built a country house. Old fruit trees on the Heidelberg Golf Course are likely related to the site of Turnbull's *"substantial good-looking country house,"* noted in McBriar's Map B. (McBriar, M. 1985)

In 1855 John T. Brown established Preston Hall Estate on part of the land. He used his 365 acres property for dairying and general agriculture and was first person in Victoria to breed Clydesdale horses. Brown built a large homestead of six rooms, on the ridge overlooking the Plenty River, which is now the site of the Heidelberg Golf Club eastern extension. It was built using handmade bricks from Scotland and featured a large overhanging verandah, with red flagstones on three sides of the house.

In 1884, Brown sold Preston Hall Estate to David Thomas, who was a partner in the Melbourne drapery firm Craig, Williamson and Thomas. Thomas died suddenly in 1887 but his widow Mary stayed on the property. She built a substantial red brick homestead next to Brown's 30 year old Preston Hall, with the two buildings connected by a walkway. (McEwan, K. 1929)

Mary Thomas called her new home Bryn Teg, meaning 'small hills' in Welsh. It had wide halls, lofty rooms, polished joinery, lead light windows, a substantial blackwood staircase and a large stained glass feature window.

A large barn was built near Bryn Teg, with the sandstone quarried from the nearby hillside. In 1920 the Lower Plenty Primary School moved from a nearby slab hut to this barn and classes were conducted there until June 1923, when the new school building was completed. (Henderson, WF. 1974)

Mary Thomas also leased part of the property to WEJ Craig, son of William Craig, one of her husband's business partners, with another shed built near the courtyard, to house his racehorses.

Mary Thomas died at Bryn Teg in August 1925. The property was sold to Heidelberg Golf House Co Ltd for the Heidelberg Golf Links in 1927. The Company had been formed in 1927 by some members of the Rosanna based Yarra Yarra Golf Club, which was relocating to Bentleigh, as they wanted to retain a golf course north of the Yarra.

They paid £13,000 for Bryn Teg, Preston Hall, 177 acres of land and the freehold title on the nearby Plenty Bridge Hotel.

Harry Alexander, the Greenkeeper from Yarra Yarra Golf Club took control on 27 June 1927 and the first 12 holes were ready by June 1928. Heidelberg Links was officially opened by the Prime Minister the Right Honourable Stanley Bruce on 23 June 1928. The full 18 holes were later opened by him on 18 April 1931. (McLachlan, I. 2017; Heidelberg Golf Club, 2021)

Bryn Teg was used as the Club House, with alterations made to meet their needs. Substantial additions were later added at each end and little remains of the original homestead's interior except for some wood work, tiled fire surrounds and the windows. Outside the imposing turreted entrance, slate roof and chimneys have been retained.

Preston Hall was initially used to house greenkeeper Harry Alexander and his family. Nothing remains of Preston Hall or the barns, though it is unclear when they were demolished. The Plenty Bridge Hotel was renamed the Golf Club Hotel, and was the Clubs 19th hole until 1936.

**Bryn Teg - Official opening of Heidelberg Links by Prime Minister Stanley Bruce, June, 1928. Source: Heidelberg Golf Club**

Official opening of Heidelberg Links by Prime Minister Stanley Bruce, June, 1928. Note Bryn Teg in right foreground with Preston Hall to left rear. Source: Heidelberg GC

Sketch of Plenty Bridge Hotel with Bryn Teg and Preston Hall to rear, and original entrance track

Preston Hall veranda in The Australian Home Beautiful Magazine June 1929. Photo by Nash Boothby.

*Walking south on the Trail, cross the pedestrian bridge over the Plenty River*

*Option 1: Turn left off the Trail just over the bridge and up to the seat, then continue south along the riverside bush track to the Melbourne Water Pipeline Reserve track and Ford*

*or*

*Option 2: continue along the Trail to Martins Lane, turn left through the gate and past the pressure release valve, along the Pipeline Reserve track to the Ford*

**Site 6: Plenty River Ford, site of the Truefitt Farm and the Melbourne Water Pipeline**

Following the Pipeline Reserve track down the hill leads to the likely site of the Ford that was used to cross the Plenty River before the construction of a bridge. During the Millennium Drought the water flow was very low and an old track wound down to the River, where you could jump across to the other side. However, a recent flood has washed away the Ford and badly eroded the western bank, leaving a steep unstable drop to the River.

On the ridge above the River, on the south side of the Pipe Track there are some remnant plantings and the remains of brick foundations and paths.

Truefitt farmhouse, Seymour Road, Viewbank. c1920s. Source: Truefitt Collection

This is the site of the Truefitt house and farm, which was located on the northern part of the original Cleveland Estate. William Truefitt, a painter and decorator, bought the property from Harold Bartram of Viewbank in the 1920s and established a chicken farm and market garden. He had married Ada Smith, a daughter of the family of WH Smith, stationers in the UK. Ada died in Lower Plenty about 1929 and William returned to the UK leaving the property in the hands of his adult sons.

The property remained in the family until after the Second World War, falling into gradual disrepair and was acquired by Parks Victoria.

Map E of the McBriar report refers to *"cleared land for cultivation"* and shows the site of buildings. (McBriar, M. 1985)

There are some ancient River Red Gums nearby and spectacular views of the Plenty River from the ridge.

Don Truefitt chopping tree near Seymour Road, 1920s

Plenty River escarpment near Truefitt house site

The location of the original slab hotel is unclear, though a possible site is the flat area above the River, on the north side of the Pipeline Track, where the earth is compacted and has only mossy ground cover.

The Melbourne Water pipeline, located under Martins Lane and the Reserve, carries water from the Silvan Reservoir to Melbourne, with a pressure release valve near the gate. The Reserve is being considered as a route for a Trail across the River to Bonds Road.

## This is as far south as the walk goes, linking into the Section 1 walk

## Follow the Pipeline Reserve track back to Martins Lane and the Plenty River Trail

Martins Lane was known as the 50 Links Wide Occupation Road in 1840. It was the boundary between Hoddles Crown Land Portion 7 to the south which became Cleveland Estate and Portion 8 to the north which became Westbank Estate, Yallambie and Woodside.

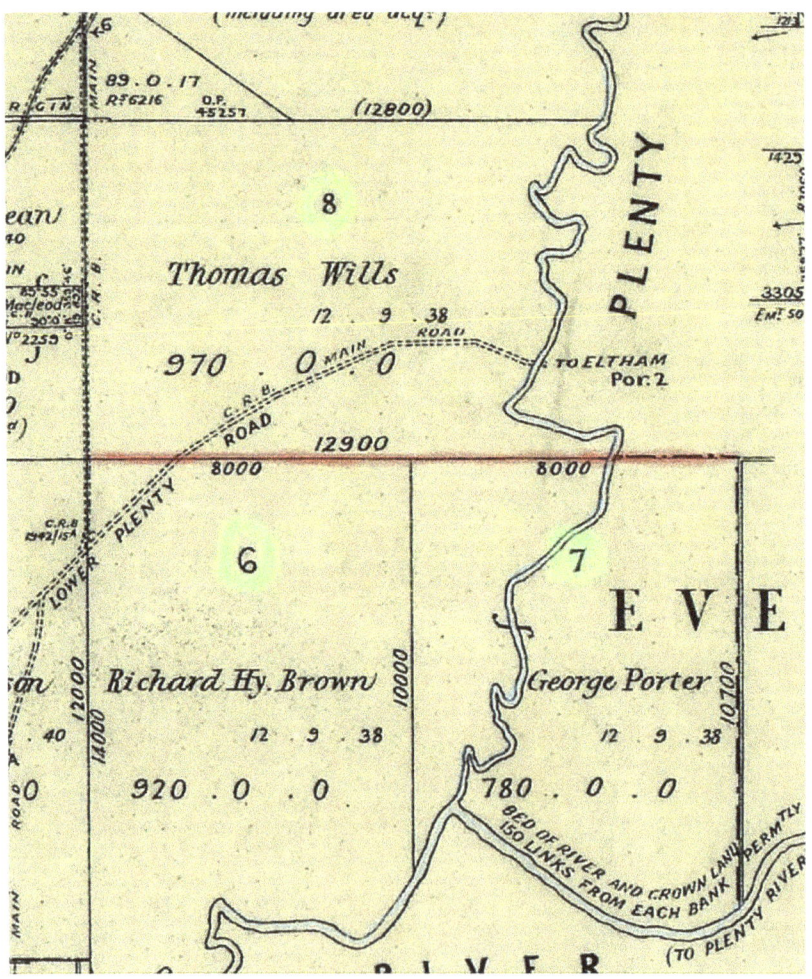

Map of Portions 6, 7 and 8 - Parish of Keelbundora 1837.
State Library Victoria (Martins Lane marked in red)

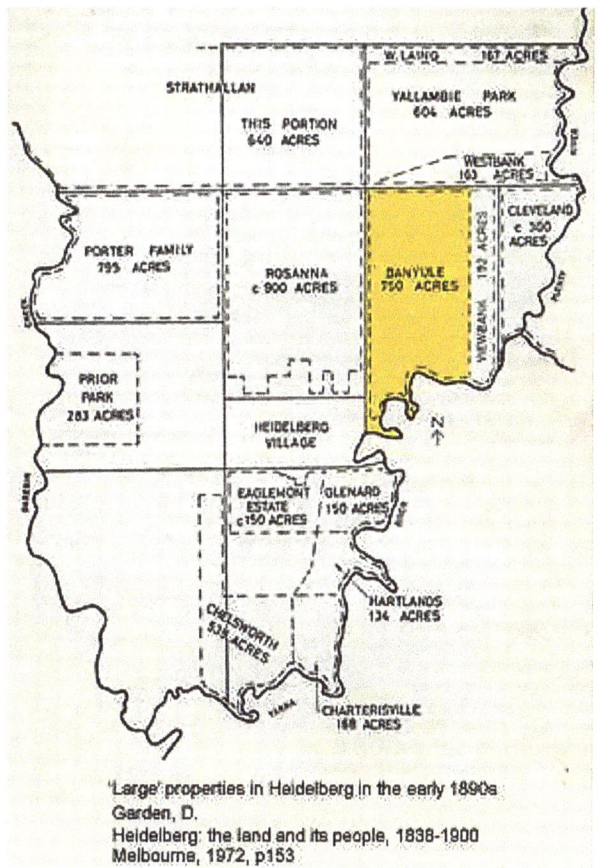

'Large' properties in Heidelberg in the early 1890s
Garden, D.
Heidelberg: the land and its people, 1838-1900
Melbourne, 1972, p153

**Subdivisions of Portion 6 and 8**
From – Garden, D. Heidelberg the Land and its People, 1972, p155

## Cleveland Estate - Crown Land Portion 7

Portion 7 was purchased by George Porter. He was a merchant and botanist and the only original purchaser to retain ownership and farm the land. After his death his sons continued as absentee landlords until they sold the property after WW1. It forms the southern boundary of the Heidelberg Golf Club, and a section now contains Rosanna Golf Club. (See Section 1 notes)

## Crown Land Portion 8

Portion 8 extended north from Martins Lane between the western bank of the Plenty River and Greensborough Road, to just north of current day Yallambie Road, on the alignment of Harborne Street to the Plenty River. This was the old City of Heidelberg - Shire of Diamond Valley boundary. Portion 8 was purchased in 1838 by Thomas Wills. He was a prominent early landowner in Port Phillip District, including Lucerne farm in Alphington (now La Trobe Golf Course) and later Willsmere in Kew.

He was the uncle of Tom Wills, the champion cricketer and co-founder of Australian football. Wills sold Portion 8 after a few months to Thomas Walker, who was a merchant banker and owned substantial land in the Heidelberg area.

### Site 7: Westbank Estate site

Westbank Estate was a 163 acre subdivision from the southern section of Portion 8, owned by Joseph Mayor Hall. It was a wedge of land extending along Martins Lane to the Plenty River, with the northern boundary near the later alignment of Old Lower Plenty Road. Hall arrived in Port Phillip District from Bristol on the ship *Lord Goderich* in 1840, with his wife Elisabeth and seven children and established his farm on the Plenty River. He was a successful cabinet maker in England and came to Victoria with stores including a dray and plough.

In 1841 Hall had a *'pretty cottage and garden'* near the Plenty River. His wife Elisabeth died in 1850 and as his older children had moved away, he moved to St Kilda with his youngest daughter Clara Ellen. He leased Westbank to cousins of the Wragges of Yallambie. (Glover, J.; McBriar, M. 1985).

Note the Parks Victoria plaque near the Trail at Martins Lane, as the likely site of Westbank Cottage.

*Follow the Plenty River Trail back to the old Bridge, cross to western side and walk a short way up Old Lower Plenty Road west to view Mollison's Lodge from the Road*

### Site 8: Mollison's Lodge

Mollison's Lodge is located near the old Bridge on Old Lower Plenty Road west. In 1915 Henry Wriedt built a retirement house on seven acres of the Westbank estate. Miss Mollison Wreidt owned the house after his death in 1924 and the property stayed in family hands until recently, when it was sold and the property subdivided for housing.

Mollison's Lodge is considered an important example of early 20$^{th}$ century pastoral buildings. It is a Federation bungalow style house with a slate roof and wide verandahs in a mature garden setting. It is privately owned and its preservation was a condition of the subdivision permit.

Mollison's Lodge in 2010, Old Lower Plenty Road

*Return to the Plenty River Trail on the west side of the old Bridge, turn left and walk under the new Main Road Bridge, toward the Plenty Station - Yallambie Park sites*

*Turn left up the SEC easement, cross Moola Avenue, and walk up to Yallambie Road. Turn right into Yallambie Road, then right again into Tarcoola Drive*

### Site 9: Plenty Station / Yallambie House - 18 Tarcoola Drive, Yallambie

In 1840 John and Robert Bakewell purchased Lot 5 of Crown Land Portion 8 for £31. Known as Plenty Station, they progressively acquired more land and by 1853 owned most of the land north of Martins Lane, to Yallambie and Greensborough Roads.

The Bakewells were partners in one of the main wool broking firms in Melbourne in the 1840s. They constructed a prefabricated timber homestead on the western ridge above the floodplain in April 1840, as well as various farm buildings. They cleared the land extensively, right down to the River bank on the Yallambie Flats and established exotic plantings, orchards and a vineyard.

> "The Plenty farm of the Bakewells is very agreeably situated on a high swell above the River. It has considerable cultivated fields, and the house is one of those wooden ones brought out from England, with thin walls and French windows ... from the lawn the bank descends steeply down a zig zag path to a flat of four or five acres which is laid out in a garden, orchards and vineyard."
>
> Howitt, R. 1855, as reported in McBriar 1985

**Painting of Plenty Station by George Gilbert in 1850, State Library of Victoria**

Plenty Station was the early name for the property but by the 1850s the Bakewells were calling it Yallambee. Thomas Wragge, who initially worked for the Bakewells, purchased the property from them in 1871 and later changed the spelling to Yallambie, to avoid confusion with another property named Yallambee.

Wragge had become a wealthy merino sheep breeder and landowner on the Wakool and Edwards Rivers of NSW. He removed most of the Bakewell buildings and built the Italianate style mansion, which remains on the site today. Wragge used Yallambie as his Melbourne base and retired there permanently until his death in 1910. The property continued to be farmed until 1959, then was progressively sold for housing. From 1938, parts of the property were also requisitioned for army training and now form the Simpson Barracks.

Yallambie House is privately owned. The house is a rare example of a 19th century Italianate building in a park setting. The garden is notable for mature trees, with a host of exotic trees associated with the original estate also scattered through adjoining properties and parkland, especially the large Bunya and Hoop pines. The landscape and house are classified by the National Trust.

**Yallambie House 1980s and 2010**

*Walking past Yallambie House, continue on to the small car park and entrance to Yallambie Park. Before entering the Laneway, look due north to the escarpment overlooking the River which is the site of Woodside / Casa Maria*

### Site 10: Woodside / Casa Maria site

Woodside was a 165 acre property, north of Yallambie, in the remainder of Portion 8. It was owned by Nicholas Fenwick in 1839 and then William Laing in 1843, whose family continued to farm the land into the 20$^{th}$ century.

The Laing house, later known as Casa Maria was built in three stages, with the first part dating back to 1839. Despite community protest and efforts to save the house, Casa Maria was demolished in 1971 during development of the Yallambie housing estate. The exotic trees on the escarpment above the River in Kurdian Court mark its location.

**Woodside / Casa Maria, photo by John T Collins 1967, State Library Victoria**

## Site 11: Laneway to Yallambie Park

The gravel laneway from the car park in Tarcoola Drive leads to Yallambie Park. It is bordered by Hawthorn and Oak trees and was the main access to the River flats for farm equipment and produce.

Yallambie Park Laneway with Oak trees

*Walking down the Laneway provides a special entry into the Yallambie Parklands*

*The Friends of the Plenty River and Banyule Council have carried out weed control and revegetation works along the Plenty River over many years, restoring important habitat in the wildlife corridor. Head south on the Trail, following the loop section beside the River*

## Site 12: Yallambie Park

Yallambie Park sits below Yallambie House and is now public parkland managed by Banyule Council. The signage on the Trail, near the loop in the River, indicates the area was a semi-permanent campsite of the Wurundjeri willam people, with good food supplies in the deep pools in the River.

The Parkland contains remnants of the Bakewell European garden and orchard plantings, with the area dominated by mature Conifers, Italian Cyprus and English Oaks.

A series of 1850s drawings by Edward La Trobe Bateman titled '*Views of Station Plenty*' capture the essence of the Bakewell landscape.

**Distant view of Station on Hill with Plenty River in foreground and Plantation of Grape Vines with Cyprus,**

**No 6 and 7 in the Plenty Station Set by Edward La Trobe Bateman 1853-56.
National Gallery of Victoria**

Of note is the magnificent Hoop Pine in the middle of Yallambie Park, along with a Bunya Pine just inside the boundary of a private property that backs onto the Park and another Hoop Pine near it, just inside the Park, beside the Plenty River Trail.

McBriar reports they were given to Wragge by Victorian Government Botanist Ferdinand von Mueller. These trees are native Queensland / NSW conifers of the Araucaria family, related to the Woolemi pine. (McBriar, M. 1985)

**Hoop Pine – Yallambie Park**

The McBriar Report also identifies the location of a Pump House and Wooden Mill near the southern end of the Yallambie Flats on the bend in the river, below the homestead and includes a sketch titled *'1859 Mill on the Plenty'*.

**1859 Mill on the Plenty, Yallambie Park from Pictorial History of Heidelberg, in McBriar Report 1985**

The 1991 Weaver Report states that the Heidelberg Heritage Committee 1987 reported:

> *"a timber mill operated by a waterwheel was built on the flat below the homestead. The mill apparently operated prior to construction of Yan Yean Reservoir. In the 1960s the foundations of the mill were visible when the river was low."*

The Report notes that no remains of the Mill were found during the archaeological survey and that a more recent pump house by the River and gardeners cottage were burnt by vandals in 1984. The Report also laments much of the orchards and walnut trees were bulldozed by Heidelberg Council in the 1980s. (Weaver, F. 1991)

Yallambie House is also visible on the ridge directly above. Note the remains of the zig zag path up to the house, referred to by Howitt in Site 8.

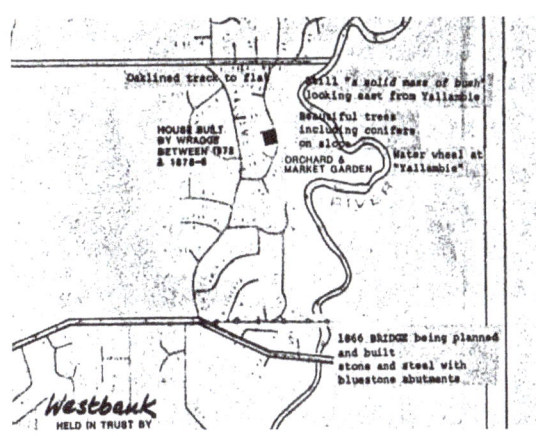

McBriar, M. 1985 Detail from Historical Map D

Yallambie and Homestead Paddock 1945

## *Continue heading south along the Plenty River Trail past the tennis courts and back under the Main Road Bridge where you can visualise how the original meandering bend in the River was eliminated to facilitate construction of the new bridge and road alignment*

You can also appreciate the integrity of the landscape, the linking of pre-European and early colonial landscape and the importance of protecting the Plenty River and its Wildlife Corridor for both its historical and environmental values.

The observations of 11 year old John Henry Howitt, when visiting his Uncle Robert Bakewell in 1842 underline this.

> *"12th April. I have been staying 3 weeks at the Plenty with Mamma and came home yesterday. I enjoyed it exceedingly. Uncle Robert made me a little carriage to ride in, and took me on several short drives in it. I went to see some trees that Willie had felled, as thick as himself which he had made a famous boast of.*
>
> *Uncle Robert has a very nice garden it is down in a flat you go to it by a zig zag walk; his vines were 14 feet high. They have abundance of Melons. The pigs are regularly fed on them and the dray and 4 bullocks brought up a load out of the garden.*
>
> *The bell birds sing all day long at the Plenty I like to hear them much better than the laughing jackasses (kookaburra)"*
>
> Howitt, JH. 1842

## *The walk concludes back at the Old Lower Plenty Road Bridge*

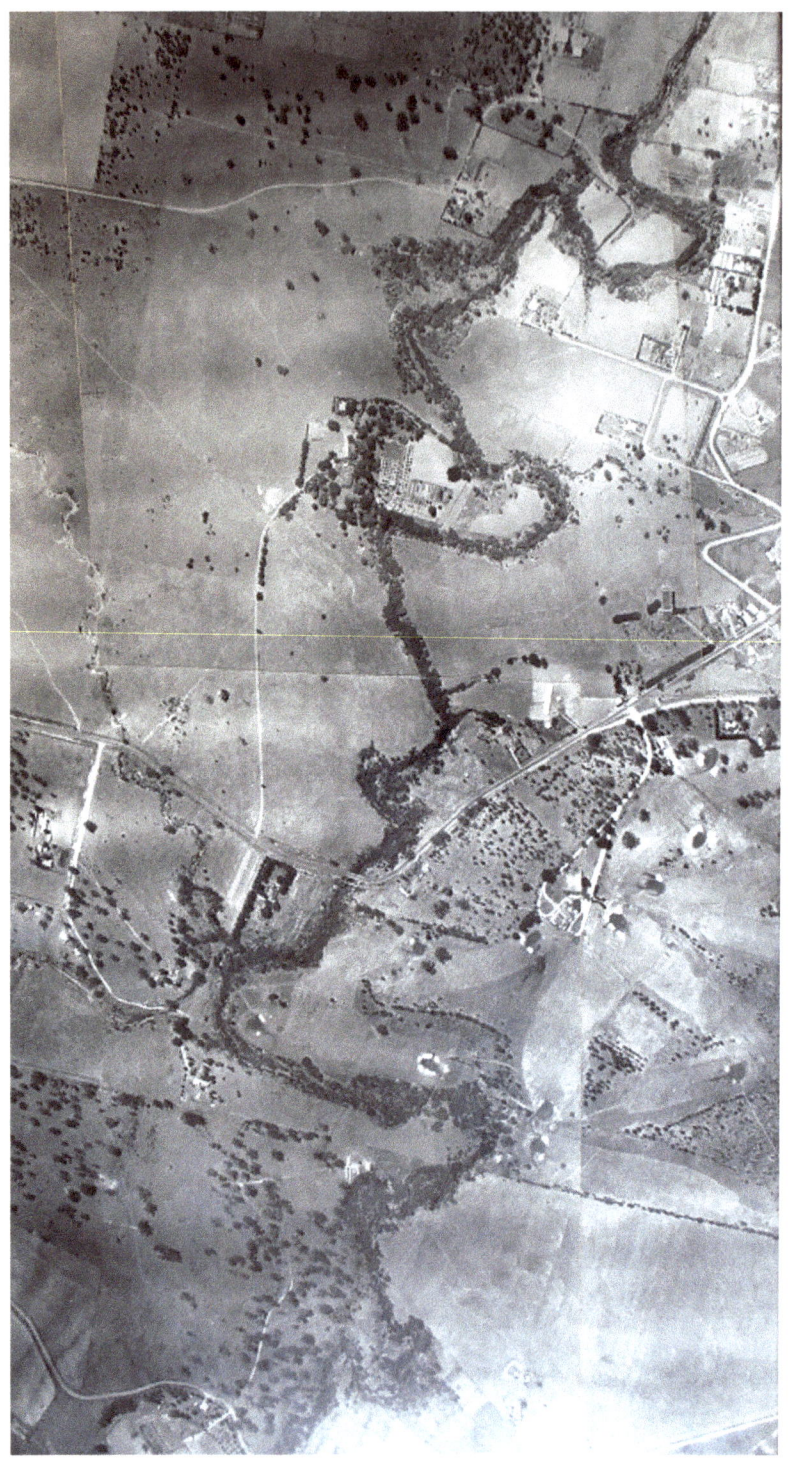

**1945 Aerial Map – Plenty River from Yarra River to Yallambie**
Source: https://1945.Melbourne

# References

Allom, Lovell and Associates, 1999 *Banyule Heritage Places Study*

Bryant, Ian. 2022. *Robert Hoddle 1837 Field Survey Notes*, unpublished research

Garden, D. 1972. *Heidelberg the Land and its People 1838-1900*. Melbourne University Press

Glover, Joan. *Pioneers of Westbank, Clara Ellen Hall*. Port Phillip Pioneers Group

Heidelberg Golf Club, 2021. *How it all Started*  https://www.heidelberggc.com.au/history/

Henderson, WF. 1974, *School at the Crossing Place, Lower Plenty. Lower Plenty Primary School 1295 1874-1974*

Howitt, John Henry. 1842 Letter to his cousin AW Howitt in England http://latrobejournal.slv.vic.gov.au/latrobejournal/issue/latrobe-27/t1-g-t2.html

Howitt, Richard. 1845 *Impressions of Australia Felix*

McBriar, M. and Loder and Bayly, 1985. *Heidelberg Conservation Study Part 2, Historical Riverland Landscape Assessment, Maps  A – E*

McEwan, Kathleen. 1929. *The Golf Clubs of Victoria* in The Australian Home Beautiful 1 June 1929

McLachlan, Ian. 2017 and 2021 *Notes on Yallambie and Truefitt farm*, https:// yallambie.wordpress.com

*Report of the Select Committee of the Legislative Council on Aborigines 1858-1859* https://aiatsis.gov.au/sites/default/files/docs/digitised_collections/remove/92768

The Argus, 1867. *Lower Plenty Road Bridge Opening, 8 March 1867*

The Argus, 1879. *Lower Plenty Toll House, 1 May 1879*

Weaver, Fiona.1991, *Lower Plenty Archaeological Survey*, MMBW. Melbourne

Willis, J. Diary, 1837, *A Pioneer Squatters Life* in Historical Records of Victoria, Volume 6, Chapter 8,

Woiwod, Mick. 2011 *Dairy of Andrew Ross 1828-1895 and Reminiscence of Andrew Ross 1851-1864*

Yeoman, R. 2013, *Notes on the Lower Plenty area*

# Images of Plenty Bridge (Golf Club) Hotel

Victorian Railways No.1 Steam Bus outside Plenty Bridge Hotel, circa 1905
Museums Victoria Collections

**Plenty Bridge Hotel and Lower Plenty Road 1940s with Irene Browne seated, daughter of owners Sidney and Ivy-Jane Browne**

Golf Club Hotel, c. pre 1936

Plenty Bridge Hotel, image courtesy Lower Plenty Hotel

Friends of Plenty
River Planting Day,
Yallambie June 2023

Plenty River Trail sign at Old
Lower Plenty Rd Bridge

Old Lower Plenty
Road Bridge 2023

www.ingramcontent.com/pod-product-compliance
Lightning Source LLC
Chambersburg PA
CBHW051318110526
44590CB00031B/4394